You Hav[e]

Have you ever travele[d] r been before and been o[verwhelmed by ...]? Do you have any irrational fears that you can't seem to explain? Are you wondering if you have a soul mate, and whether or not you'll ever meet him or her?

Although our modern Western culture does not readily accept the idea of reincarnation, it is likely that irrational fears, strange feelings of déjà vu, or a fascination with a long-lost time and place may be related to events that happened in a past life. Past-life memories can be the key to unlocking the secret fears and motivations that may be hindering your progress in your current life.

Popular metaphysical author and hypnotherapist Richard Webster has regressed hundreds of people to their past lives. He has seen firsthand the dramatic effects that the events and traumas of the past can often carry over into a current lifetime. Based on his work, he has developed twelve methods anyone can use to access past-life memories. Each method is presented here along with detailed case histories and examples from his private practice.

Gain a new perspective on life and death, and a greater sense of your purpose in this life with the knowledge that you have lived before.

About the Author

Richard Webster was born in New Zealand in 1946 and he resides there still. He travels widely every year, lecturing and conducting workshops on psychic subjects around the world. He has written many books, mainly on psychic subjects, and also writes monthly magazine columns. Richard is married with three children. His family is very supportive of his occupation, but his oldest son, after watching his father's career, has decided to become an accountant.

Many of Llewellyn's authors have websites with additional information and resources. For more information, please visit our website at http://www.llewellyn.com.

Practical Guide to

PAST-LIFE MEMORIES

Twelve Proven Methods

RICHARD WEBSTER

2001
Llewellyn Publications
St. Paul, Minnesota 55164-0383, U.S.A.

First Edition
First Printing, 2001

Book layout and editing by Joanna Willis
Book design by Pam Keesey and Kimberly Nightingale
Cover design by William Merlin Cannon

Library of Congress Cataloging-in-Publication Data
Webster, Richard, 1946–
    Practical guide to past-life memories: twelve proven methods / Richard Webster.—1st ed.
        p.   cm.
    Includes bibliographical references and index.
    ISBN 0-7387-0077-0
    1. Reincarnation. I. Title.

BL515 .W43 2001
133.9'01'35—dc21

2001038330

Llewellyn Publications
A Division of Llewellyn Worldwide, Ltd.
P.O. Box 64383, Dept. 0-7387-0077-0
St. Paul, MN 55164-0383, U.S.A.
www.llewellyn.com

Printed in the United States of America

Other Books by Richard Webster

For my good friend Blair Robertson,
Canada's leading hypnotist.

Contents

Introduction

Infinite time, without beginning and without end,
hath been given to me; I inherit eternity and ever-
lastingness hath been bestowed upon me.

Egyptian Book of the Dead (c. 1450 B.C.E.)

It must have been at least a quarter of a century ago, but I remember it as if it happened
last week. My client, a middle-aged woman,
lay on my recliner chair while I regressed her
back to her childhood to see if we could determine the underlying reason behind her weight
problem.

This is a standard procedure with people who are seriously overweight. Usually we are able to return to whatever it was that started the pattern of steady weight gain. And once the person realizes what it was, and is able to release it, the weight would then start to come off, and stay off.

Usually the incident would be a trifling one that occurred in childhood or adolescence. It was invariably a painful situation at the time, but one that had been consciously forgotten. Returning to it, and looking at it from the standpoint of a mature adult, allows my clients to realize that they no longer need to carry it, and their excess weight, around with them anymore. Consequently, it is an extremely effective technique.

"I'd like you to go back now," I told my client, "to the very first situation that started your weight problems. You will find it easy to do, and you will remain detached and calm, no matter what situation you find yourself in. Drifting back now, drifting back through time and space to the very first incident that relates to your reasons for being here today."

"I'm there." My client's voice had become deeper and even though she was resting quietly in my chair, her body language appeared to have changed subtly.

"Where are you?"

"They're fighting."

My first thought was that her parents had been squabbling, but it pays to take nothing for granted. "Who is fighting?" I asked.

"Everyone. All the grown-ups. It's noisy and there are fires. Dead people everywhere."

This was not a normal regression. The woman was too young to have been involved in the Second World War, and I could not think of another conflict that she might have been involved in.

"Where are you?" I asked.

"Home." The woman's face crumpled and she began to cry.

I immediately told her to step back and look at the scene in a detached manner, as if it was happening to someone else.

"My home's gone," she said between tears. "The street, the town, it's all gone. Just the fighting. And then it's all still. And there's no one, just me."

"What country are you in?" I asked, still thinking she was talking about an event from this lifetime. She shook her head and sighed.

"What year are you living in?" I continued. Again, I got no answer.

Gradually the weeping ceased and she began to talk. Both her parents were killed in the fighting, and she had no idea what had happened to her brothers and sisters. Her town had been destroyed, and she and a few other survivors lived on whatever scraps of food they could find. It was unbearably hot during the day and incredibly cold at night. Soon the food ran out, and she eventually died of starvation.

She was calm when I brought her back to the present. She did not appear at all surprised that she had returned to a past life. I had to give the impression that this happened all the time, even though it was the first time I had experienced the phenomenon.

Instead, we talked about the situation she had uncovered and how it related to her current weight problems. Obviously, as she had died of starvation in a previous lifetime, she was subconsciously determined that this would never occur again and ate whatever food was placed in front of her. Once she realized this, her excess weight fell off and she became a wonderful advertisement for my hypnotherapy practice.

This example is an extreme one. Usually when I regress someone back to their childhood, the initial incident is a trivial one from an adult perspective. It may have been a careless remark by which nothing was even meant. One client of mine regressed back to a time she was out with her father and saw some prostitutes wearing brightly colored clothes.

"Look at the pretty ladies," she said.

Her father turned to look and was horrified. He yanked his daughter's arm. "Don't look at them," he said. From this incident the young girl learned that her father did not like beautiful ladies and became over-weight in an attempt to please him. Naturally, once this long-forgotten memory returned, my client was able to see why she had put on weight and was then able to lose it permanently.

Over the years many people have spontaneously returned to their past lives while in my office. Some-times this has been an alarming experience, particularly for people who had given no previous thought to the possibility of past lives. But it was that first spontaneous past-life regression that caused me to change the emphasis of my hypnotherapy practice and become a past-life specialist. I was interested in the subject anyway, and have a number of memories that do not relate to the experiences of my present life. The concept of reincarnation always seemed a highly logical one to me.

I quickly found that there was no single method that worked with everyone. I love hypnosis, but I came to realize that not everyone shares my enthusiasm for it. Many people have a variety of fears about hypnotism. They think they might lose control, blurt out some guilty secret, or perhaps do something they would never do normally. None of these things are possible, but if the subject thinks they are, hypnosis cannot be induced.

Also, not everyone regresses to a past life. There are three possible reasons for this. The first of these is fear. If someone is terrified of what they might experience, or perhaps has religious hang-ups concerning reincarnation, he or she will not relax enough to allow the past-life memories to flow. Also, if there is no rapport between the subject and the hypnotist, the subject may not relax enough to allow it to happen.

A second possible reason is that the person may not have had any previous lifetimes. In this case, he or she is a "new soul" and has not been here before. I have yet to find anyone who is here for the first time. I believe that all souls were created at the same time, but have developed at different rates since then.

A final possible reason is that the events of the most recent past life were so traumatic that the person's subconscious mind has deliberately closed them off, and in the process closed off access to all earlier lives as well. This is particularly likely if the person experienced a horrific death.

Consequently, I have experimented with many different methods of helping people return to their past lives over the years. I had to find different techniques to use with people who would not allow themselves to be hypnotized, or who did not recall any previous lifetimes while in a state of hypnosis. I have included the most effective of those methods here. Everyone is different, and you will find that some of the techniques explained in this book work better for you than others. Read the whole book first, and decide which ones appeal to you most. These are likely to be the methods that work best for you.

If you want to unlock your long-forgotten memories of previous lifetimes, you will be able to do so using the techniques explained here.

1

Your Many Past Lives

Birth is not a beginning; death is not an end.

Chuang Tzu (369?–286? B.C.E.)

"My husband and I went on a camping trip last summer. We had never done anything like it before, and I found it hard to fall asleep outdoors under the stars. It was beautiful lying there in my husband's arms, but once he fell asleep I'd lie there for hours, half expecting an attack at any moment. Three days into the vacation I managed to fall asleep in the middle of the night and dreamt that I was a young American Indian boy lost in the same area we were camping in. I could feel the young boy's nervousness and fear as he

1

struggled to find food and make his way home. He lay on the ground at night, just as I was doing, and he wasn't able to sleep either as he was aware of every sound and movement. He seemed to think he was being followed or pursued, and all day long he kept looking behind him. He did this day after day. Eventually, it all got to be too much for him and he began to run. He caught his foot in the root of a tree and fell, breaking a leg. He couldn't move, and he lay on the ground waiting for death. When I woke up, I was sweating and my heart was racing. I'm convinced that I was that boy. It was far too vivid and real to be a dream."

"All my life I've had this strange feeling of forboding, as if something bad is about to happen. Last year I visited Athens for the first time and when I went to the Parthenon the feeling totally overcame me. I collapsed onto the steps, tears rolling down my face. People came up and asked if they could help, but there was nothing I could tell them. All I know is that I had been there before. Not in this lifetime, but in another life. Something bad happened to me in the Parthenon and visiting it again released all of those feelings I've always had. Since that day I've been totally free of them. I'm not sure if I really want to find out what happened in that past life."

"My brothers and sisters learned to swim easily, but I was always terrified of water. It made my father furious as we were a boating family and spent all our vacations either on or beside the ocean. When I was thirteen my parents took me to a hypnotist for nail-biting. While there, I spontaneously regressed to a past life on a small Pacific island. It was a good life, and we made our living catching fish. One day we were racing home ahead of a storm, but got caught up in it. I fell overboard, and even though I was a strong swimmer, I drowned. I had never given reincarnation a thought until then. The hypnotist explained it all to me, but I never told my parents about it as it seemed so strange. The weirdest part was that my wife in that past life is my mother in this life. That confused me for years."

Have you ever wondered about your past lives? Many people do. For some this interest is sparked by a vague, faint memory they have of something that happened in the past. For others it's a desire to know more about themselves—where they have been and where they are going. No matter what your reasons may be, you can successfully explore your own past lives.

People have believed in the concept of reincarnation for thousands of years. Belief in reincarnation is universal too. People in Asia, the Americas, Africa, Australasia, and Europe all believe that death is not the end, and that we will be reborn into another body.

In the East reincarnation has always been taken for granted. It is an essential part of Hinduism, Buddhism, Jainism, and Sikhism. It was not originally part of Shintoism, but once Buddhism reached Japan in the twelfth century it gradually became part of the belief system there. Reincarnation is not part of Islamic beliefs but the Sufi sect does accept the concept of rebirth.

The ancient Egyptians buried magic spells with the deceased to enable them to be reborn in whatever form they chose. In Greece in the sixth century B.C.E., the Orphic cult taught that we are all part evil and part divine. And as we progress through different incarnations we learn to eliminate the evil side of our natures and ultimately become divine. At this stage, of course, the cycle of rebirth is complete.[1]

The ideas of the Orphics were later adopted by Pythagoras and became an integral part of his philosophy. Pythagoras was able to recall his previous lives. Iamblichus, in his *Life of Pythagoras,* wrote, "What Pythagoras wished to indicate by all these particulars was that he knew the former lives he had lived, which enabled him to bring providential attention to others and remind them of their former existences."[2] Pythagoras remembered lives as the Trojan warrior Euphorbus, as the prophet Hermotimus who was burned to death by his rivals, as the Cypriot fisherman Pyrrhus, as a prostitute in Phoenicia, a peasant in Thrace, and the wife of a shopkeeper in Thrace.[3]

Socrates, too, believed in reincarnation strongly. He is believed to have spent the last morning of his life thinking about how the soul existed before someone was born and will continue to live after the physical body has died. Socrates used philosophy to analyze human life, which is where his most famous saying— "Know thyself"—comes from. His original ideas about the soul are still being discussed today.

Socrates' most famous pupil, Plato, was a firm believer in reincarnation and wrote, "Know that if you become worse you will go to the worse souls, or if better to the better, and in every succession of life and death you will do and suffer what like may fitly suffer at the hands of like."[4] Plato's ideas on reincarnation had a profound effect on Western philosophy that is still present today.

Later still, Greek Gnosticism adopted the concept of reincarnation. It played an important role in early Christian beliefs. In the second century C.E., Clement of Alexandria wrote that we developed through a process of many incarnations. Origen, one of the most important theologians of the day, agreed with him.

A number of passages in the Bible appear to take the concept of reincarnation for granted. In Matthew 11:13–15 Jesus tells his disciples who John the Baptist had been in a previous life: "For all the prophets and the law prophesied until John. And if ye will receive it, this is Elias, which was for to come. He that hath ears to hear, let him hear." This statement is confirmed in Matthew 17:12 where Jesus says, "But I say unto you, that Elias is come already, and they knew him not, but have done unto him whatsoever they listed. Likewise shall also the Son of man suffer of them." On another occasion Jesus asked his disciples, "Who do men say that I the Son of man am?" The reply was, "Some say that thou art John the Baptist; some Elias; and others Jeremias, or one of the prophets" (Matthew 16:13–14).

The disciples make another reference to reincarnation when they ask Jesus about a man who had been blind from birth: "And his disciples asked him, saying, Master, who did sin, this man, or his parents, that he was born blind?" (John 9:2). Obviously, it would have been impossible for this man to have sinned before he was born, unless he had sinned in a previous life. Interestingly, Jesus does not rebuke his disciples for thinking in this way: "Jesus answered, 'Neither hath this man sinned, nor his parents, but that the works of God should be made manifest in him'" (John 9:3).

Unfortunately, in 553 C.E. the Council of Constantinople declared that reincarnation was a heretical doctrine. The Christian Church immediately renounced the concept of reincarnation and forced its believers underground. Reincarnation was again considered heretical by both the Council of Lyons in 1274 and the Council of Florence in 1493. Anyone believing in reincarnation risked being burned at the stake.

Despite this, belief in reincarnation did not disappear. Possibly the most famous of these underground sects were the Cathars who were destroyed by the Inquisition. Interestingly, the only references to reincarnation in the Bible are favorable ones.[5]

During the Renaissance in Europe there was an upsurge of interest in the ideas of Pythagoras, the Kabbalah, and Platonism. Leonardo da Vinci was one of many people who accepted the concept of reincarnation. His *Notebooks* include several passages expressing his belief that the soul was eternal. Also, when Giordano Bruno was found guilty of heresy and was to be put to death in 1600, he told the Inquisition, "I have held and hold souls to be immortal. . . . Since the soul is not found without body and yet is not body, it may be in one body or in another, and pass from body to body."[6]

The concept of reincarnation can be found in the Jewish Kabbalah[7] and the Zohar.[8] There are also numerous mentions of reincarnation in the Indian Bhagavad Gita and Upanishads, and the references to it in the Islamic Koran are favorable ones.[9] In Buddhism the ultimate aim is to be freed from the endless cycle of rebirth and to achieve nirvana. In fact, the concept of reincarnation, or a variant of it, can be found in the traditions of most people throughout the world.

Interest in reincarnation grew steadily throughout the eighteenth and nineteenth centuries. Benjamin Franklin and Thomas Paine wrote on the subject in America. At the same time Voltaire, Victor Hugo, George Sand, and Gustave Flaubert in France, Johann von Goethe,

Immanuel Kant, and Gotthold Lessing in Germany, and David Hume and Alexander Pope in England were educating the public about it in Europe.

The modern-day revival of interest in reincarnation began with the work of the Theosophical Society. The Theosophical Society was intended to be a universal brotherhood that promoted the study of comparative religion, philosophy, and science, and investigated the unexplained laws in nature. Today, the society promotes no specific dogmas, but tends to accept the reality of reincarnation and karma. The Theosophical Society was founded in 1875 by Madame Helena Blavatsky, Henry Olcott, and William Judge. Madame Blavatsky claimed that she had been Pythagoras and Paracelsus in previous incarnations.

In more modern times, Edgar Cayce (1877–1945), a committed Christian, became a major advocate of reincarnation. Initially he was concerned when he mentioned reincarnation and karma while in a trance. He had not previously heard of karma and thought that reincarnation was something taught by heathens. Fortunately, Cayce's friends encouraged him to carry on with his work, and after some experimentation he came to the conclusion that there was nothing heathen or bad about what he was doing. In fact, his ability to look into people's past lives enabled him to be much more effective than ever before as he was able to treat both the bodies and minds of his patients. Between 1923 and 1945 Cayce gave some 2,500 life readings, all of which are preserved at the Association for Research and Enlightenment at Virginia Beach.[10] These readings vividly show how people's attitudes and personalities change and develop as they progress from one life to another.

Interest in reincarnation grew steadily throughout the twentieth century. Alexander Cannon, a British psychiatrist, and Colonel Albert de Rochas, a French psychic pioneer, explored hypnotic regressions in the early years of the century. Even Aleister Crowley wrote a book on his method of recalling past lives. In the 1950s the famous Bridey Murphy case in the United States, followed by the past-life memories of Mrs. Naomi Henry in England, created enormous excitement and interest. These memories were uncovered by hypnosis.

A Welsh hypnotherapist named Arnall Bloxham had also been exploring past-life hypnotic regressions for many years, and recorded more than four hundred of his sessions. Jeffrey Iverson, the producer of a television show about the Bloxham tapes, later wrote a book called *More Lives than One* that became a bestseller in 1976.

In 1983 *Out on a Limb,* Shirley MacLaine's first book on reincarnation, was published. It was so popular that it became the subject of a TV miniseries. Her books are easy to read and have done more to introduce reincarnation to the general public than anything else.

In the 1970s Dr. Helen Wambach hypnotically regressed more than one thousand people and gathered a huge amount of data that vividly demonstrates the reality of reincarnation. With one exception, all of her volunteers were regular people in previous lifetimes who led normal, everyday lives. Most of them were peasants who led lives of incredible hardship. They worked hard and existed on a meager diet of dull food. Many of their children died as babies or infants. These are not the sort of lives that people would take themselves back to if they were simply fantasizing.

Dr. Wambach also found that although most of her volunteers were white and middle-class, they frequently became members of races and sexes other than their own when they were taken back to past lifetimes. Also, as there are an approximately equal number of men and women in the world at any given time, you would expect this proportion to remain constant when one thousand people are regressed. This, in fact, is the case. Of the 1,100 past lives Helen Wambach examined, 49.4 percent were women and 50.6 percent men.[11] It has been said that if these regressions were purely fantasies, most people would choose to be white males.[12] The fact that this is not the case further indicates that these are genuine memories of previous lives.

Dr. Wambach's research also answers another important question. Doesn't the fact that the world's population is steadily increasing disprove the theory of reincarnation? Dr. Wambach found that her subjects went back to specific periods in history in exactly the same degree of frequency that would occur if reincarnation were an established fact. The population of the world doubled between the first and fifteenth centuries, doubled again by the nineteenth, and has quadrupled since then. Dr. Wambach's subjects returned to past lives at exactly the same rate.

More than half of the world's population takes the concept of reincarnation for granted. They accept that the human body, with its personality and other characteristics, will die, but that the soul itself is immortal, has lived many previous lifetimes, and will experience many more in the future.

This is perfectly natural as it is impossible to experience everything in just one lifetime. However over a series of lifetimes we can experience lives in many different ways: we can be both rich and poor, black and white, male and female, intellectually brilliant and mentally handicapped, radiantly healthy and crippled with illness. We can live in countries that are technologically advanced, and again in places where it is a struggle simply to survive. In effect, we are each other. If nothing else, knowledge of reincarnation is likely to make people more tolerant of others.

Over a period of many incarnations we gradually progress or regress, depending on our thoughts and actions in each lifetime. This is the law of cause and effect. We all reap exactly what we sow.

Why Do People Not Remember Their Past Lives?

The ancient Greeks believed that the gods dipped the souls who were about to be reborn in the River of Forgetfulness to ensure that all memories of past lives were lost. In fact, it is probably fortunate that most people have no recall of their past lives. All the painful and difficult memories of previous lives would make forward progress in this current life next to impossible.

Most people are born with no conscious memories of their past incarnations. However, many people recall glimpses of their past lives, sometimes in great detail. All my life I have had memories of being a small child sitting beside a huge bonfire with a full stomach watching large circles of red going around and around. As an adult I discovered that the circles of red were the inside linings of the black dresses that Russian peasant women wore. As they danced around the fire, all I could see were the circles of red. Obviously that was a past-life memory, but it was only a partial recall of a happy moment. I had to reach adulthood to uncover more of this past life.

Not surprisingly, people who remember their past lives are found more frequently in countries where reincarnation is accepted as a fact. A survey conducted in northern India in the 1970s showed "that about one person in five hundred claimed to remember a previous life."[13] There have been no similar surveys in the West.

Dr. Ian Stevenson has spent the last forty years investigating cases "of the reincarnation type," and has written a series of well-documented books about his findings. Over the years he has recorded more than 2,500 cases, mainly involving the past-life memories of young children. Some eight hundred of these cases have been investigated and analyzed.

Dr. Stevenson believes that the evidence of young children is more convincing than that of adults. This is because they have not had time to read historical novels or see many films or television programs that they could unwittingly regurgitate as evidence of a past life. The act of remembering buried and forgotten memories lying just under the surface of our minds is known as *cryptomnesia*. Dr. Stevenson believes that most hypnotic regressions bring back these forgotten memories, rather than genuine past lives.

One case that has been thoroughly investigated by Professor Stevenson and many others is the case of Parmod, the second son of a college professor in India. Parmod was born in 1944, and as soon as he was able to talk he said the words "Moradabad," "Saharanpur," and "Mohan Brothers." When he was two and a half years old he told his mother that she did not need to cook as he had a wife in Moradabad. When his relatives bought biscuits, he told them that he owned a large biscuit factory in Moradabad. He repeatedly asked to go to Moradabad and said that he was one of the Mohan Brothers. As time went on, more details emerged. He said his name was Paramanand, a businessman who had died just nine months and six days before his birth as Parmod.

When Parmod was five, a friend of the family discovered that there was a company known as Mohan Brothers in Moradabad. When Mohan Lal, the owner of this business, heard about Parmod, he paid a visit to the boy's home in Bissauli. Unfortunately, Parmod was away visiting relatives, but arrangements were made for him to visit Moradabad.

When the family arrived in Moradabad, Parmod immediately recognized his brother and embraced him warmly. He recognized the town hall and announced that they were close to the shop. The vehicle they were in deliberately drove past the shop to test Parmod, but he recognized the building and ordered the driver to stop. He went into the house that he had lived in in his previous life, and showed reverence in the room that he had previously reserved for his daily devotions. He recognized his wife, parents, brothers, and all of his children except for his oldest son. This son, however, was thirteen when Paramanand died, and had changed enormously during the six years since they had last seen each other. Parmod joyfully recalled incidents about the family and their life together.

During the two days he spent in Moradabad, Parmod effectively proved that he was the reincarnation of Paramanand by recognizing different places and people that he had known in his previous life. He was able to point out a building that had once been a branch office of Mohan Brothers. He was able to explain how to make aerated water, and knew why the machine would not work. It had been deliberately tampered with to test him.[14]

Small children often show a specific talent or aptitude at an extremely young age. This is most likely the result of past-life experiences. The rich imagination of small children can also indicate memories of previous incarnations.

One problem people have with hypnotic past-life regressions is that they can seldom be verified. Someone may tell a wonderful story full of incredible detail that can be confirmed about a previous life. However, doubt lingers that maybe he or she somehow learned the information in this lifetime, perhaps by reading a book or watching a film. This problem does not exist when small children recall memories of their past lives as there is no possibility that they learned the information in any other way.

In the West, children who recall past lives are told to stop making things up, or are considered to be playing an imaginary game. As these children mature their memories gradually fade until they are completely lost.

Is It Dangerous?

There is no danger whatsoever in undertaking a past-life regression using the techniques in this book. However, there are other methods that are potentially dangerous. In the 1970s many people explored their past lives with the help of various drugs. Not surprisingly, some of these people had unfortunate experiences. There is no need for artificial stimulants to successfully explore your past lives.

There are also methods of returning to your past lives using body work. In this method, someone touches various parts of your body to see what responses are created. When the right spot is touched, you return to a past life. This is an effective method that I have used many times, but I have not included it here for two reasons. I have heard stories of people taking advantage of others during the process. Obviously, you need to trust the person who is doing the touching. The other disadvantage is that you cannot use this method on your own. None of the methods explained in this book require a partner.

There is something else to be considered. Becoming aware of our past lives also makes us aware of the karma created in those lifetimes. This knowledge can be difficult for some people to handle. Most of us are struggling with the karma created by our present life without having to worry about the karma created in previous lives. Consequently, it is better not to undertake a past-life regression unless you are certain that you will be able to handle whatever comes up.

In practice I have found that most people have no difficulties returning to their previous lifetimes. However, a few people try every method and still fail to unlock the door to their past incarnations. I feel that this is deliberate; that they are being prevented from recalling their past lives until they are ready to receive the information.

Why Explore Your Past Lives?

People frequently ask me why anyone would want to explore their past lives. My usual reply is that a past-life regression can provide valuable clues as to why a person acts and behaves in certain ways in this present lifetime. A past-life regression can often provide information as to what the person's purpose in this life is. It can explain the reasons behind difficulties and problems he or she has in this life and clue one in to what karma needs to be repaid. When people know why they act and react in certain ways they gain much more control over their lives.

Past-life therapy is also an extremely valuable form of healing. It allows you to deal with the underlying causes of a problem rather than try to deal with the symptoms. The memories of our past lives are imprinted in the DNA of every one of the more than ten trillion cells that make up our bodies.[15] When we utilize past-life healing techniques we can heal "dis-ease" that may have existed for many previous lifetimes.

Guilt plays a major role in many people's lives. Suppressed fear, anger, and grief all create feelings of guilt. Past-life therapy can help these people let go of guilt that was created in previous incarnations.

Many people choose to have a past-life regression when they are at a moment of crisis. When everything seems to be going wrong in their lives, many people search for a solution in previous lifetimes. Regardless of what is uncovered, these regressions always appear to be beneficial.

One lady came to me shortly after her partner had left her. "I've always been jealous," she told me. "I don't know why. It's so crazy because I always end up losing the people I love the most."

She went back to a life in nineteenth-century Jamaica. She was the spoiled elder daughter of rich plantation owners and always received whatever she wanted. She fell in love with a young man, but unfortunately he was in love with someone else. She tried everything she could to woo him away from the girl he loved, but nothing worked. In a fit of jealousy she paid someone to poison her rival. When he heard that the girl he loved was dead, the young man hanged himself.

After this regression my client went for further counseling. Although her partner did not return to her, she is getting on with her life and tells me that her feelings of jealousy occur only occasionally.

Possibly the most important thing that can be gained from a past-life regression is forgiveness, both for yourself and others. You can forgive the people who harmed you in previous lifetimes, and you can also forgive yourself for the things that you did to others. This creates an unconditional acceptance of yourself and others. When this state is reached, your progress will be a joy to behold.

Greater peace of mind is also a main benefit of learning about your previous lives. Many people fear death, and this fear vanishes once they realize that death is not the end.

Another advantage to past-life regression is discovering talents that you did not know you had. The skills and talents that you used in previous lifetimes have not been lost. They are still part of you and can be developed further in this lifetime once you become aware of them.

Most people, however, who choose to have a past-life regression do so to find out if they are fulfilling their true purpose in this lifetime. Many people feel unfulfilled and want to find out what they should be doing with their lives. A past-life regression can be extremely helpful in this regard. If nothing else, it proves that our potential is unlimited.

Most of my clients have expressed a belief in reincarnation, but some remain skeptical even after experiencing a regression. However, regardless of their views on the subject, they have all been helped in some way by becoming exposed to one of their many past lives. Whether your interest is serious or casual, you will find the experiments in the following chapters interesting and beneficial to you in this lifetime.

Does Everyone Have a Past Life?

I have yet to experience a situation in which someone came to me for a past-life regression and failed to have any past lives at all. In fact, most people appear to have a limitless number to choose from.

One of my regular clients is a carpenter. Over a period of almost twenty years we have explored scores of his past lives. Sometimes when he comes to visit me he will want to explore a particular past life we have already uncovered in greater detail. At other times he might want to look at a past life he is not already familiar with. Sometimes he leaves it to chance.

One common factor in his many past lives is that he has always been good with his hands. He seems to have had at least as many lives as a female as he has experienced as a male, but in all of them his dexterity has been utilized. In his male incarnations he has been a builder, cabinet maker, road builder, farmer, mechanic, and so on. In his female incarnations he has been a cowherd, cook, nurse, and cleaner.

I find the thread of practicality running through all of his lives fascinating as my own past lives have been the complete opposite. I am basically impractical, and in most of my past lives I have been a monk, preacher, musician, writer, or teacher.

Unfortunately, many of my clients come to me out of curiosity and do not carry on to explore multiple lifetimes, as my carpenter client has, once this curiosity has been satisfied. Consequently, I do not know if most people have a common thread running through their different incarnations. It is an interesting field of inquiry.

I do know, however, that you have experienced many past lives. You have been here many times before, and will return here again many times in the future.

What About Déjà Vu?

Virtually everyone has experienced déjà vu at some time or another. This French expression means "already seen." It is the feeling that one has been to a place or experienced a certain sensation or sequence of events before when you know that you have not. Reincarnation is just one of many possible explanations for this. Other explanations include having seen the scene on television before, seeing a scene that is similar but not identical, or even dreaming of the event before it happened.

Sometimes, however, déjà vu leads to a spontaneous recall of a past life. This can be surprising for people who have not previously given the subject any thought.

A lady I know experienced this one evening at home. She had cut up some lemon to put in the drinks she prepared for her husband and herself, and then sat down on the veranda in front of their house to watch the sun set. As she raised her glass to her lips she smelled the lemon on her fingers and was instantly transported back to a past life in Renaissance Italy where she was posing for a painting in a large garden.

"I am sure it was lemon balm in the garden," she told me. "But the smell of lemon suddenly took me back. I have no idea why it happened at that particular moment, as I've known the scent of lemon all my life. Anyway, I was blissfully happy. I was in love with Aroldo, who I was posing for, and I felt a surge of joy so great that I felt my heart would burst." She smiled ruefully. "I've never experienced anything like that in this lifetime."

Dr. Frederick Lenz is a psychologist who has studied spontaneous past-life recall. He describes his findings in his book titled *Lifetimes*. Dr. Lenz found that most spontaneous past-life memories came back as dreams, or while the person was meditating, as a waking vision, or from experiences with déjà vu. Dr. Lenz found that immediately before a spontaneous past-life recall these people would feel that they were becoming lighter and bright colors would flicker in front of their eyes. They would experience a euphoric feeling of well-being and the room would appear to vibrate. Then they would suddenly be transported back to a past life for a few moments. Often they appeared slightly dazed once the experience was over.

Can I Prove That a Past Life Really Happened?

Unfortunately, this is not possible in most cases. Most people lived average lives in the time period that they lived in. Few had the opportunity to receive an education or to travel. Consequently, their lives were spent in a small area close to their home. They may not have known the name of the nearest town or village. It is unlikely that they would have known the year they were born in, or the name of the country they lived in. They may not even have known their own last name. Naturally, it is impossible to prove or disprove these stories.

Just recently I regressed a young woman back to medieval Europe. She was a man in that lifetime and worked as a baker. He was ambitious, worked hard, and ultimately owned his own business. The amount of detail that came through about baking bread was incredible. However, he was illiterate and had no idea of the date or even the name of the town he lived in. Obviously, it would be extremely hard to find out more about him, as he knew so little himself.

At other times a wealth of detail may emerge but cannot be proved because of the absence of historical records. Jess Stearn explored one of these cases in his book *The Search for the Girl with the Blue Eyes.* The girl with blue eyes lived in rural Canada in the late nineteenth century. She never went far from her home, knew few of her neighbors, and lived in a time when records of births, deaths, and marriages were scant or nonexistent. Although the story is extremely convincing and contains a wealth of detail, it still fails to prove the reality of reincarnation.

Another example that was exhaustively researched concerns George Field, a fifteen-year-old high-school boy who regressed back to a lifetime as a farmer during the Civil War. When he refused to sell his potatoes to Yankee soldiers for a few cents a bushel, he was shot in the stomach and died. The regression was conducted by Loring G. Williams who later wrote an account of it for *Fate* magazine. Further information came to light after the article was published and was included in Brad Steiger's fascinating book *You Will Live Again.*[16] Williams traveled to Jefferson, North Carolina, with George Field in search of verification. George Field, or Jonathan Powell, which was his name in this earlier life, was able to provide a great deal of information about people living in the area at the time. Yet, although a large amount of information was able to be verified, it still failed to conclusively prove the reality of past-life regressions.

Every now and again one of my clients will return to a lifetime as a person we can research further in history books. I regressed someone back to a lifetime in which he was a bookkeeper for Oliver Cromwell. Upon checking history books we learned that someone of the same name was indeed Oliver Cromwell's bookkeeper. He remembered this lifetime in great detail and even used terms that are not familiar today. Consequently, it is possible, even highly likely, that my client was this person in a previous lifetime.

Unfortunately, it is impossible to prove that this is the case. Skeptics rightly say that my client may have picked up the information from a long-forgotten book that he read. He may have heard a radio program or seen a film or television drama in which this person was featured. Therefore, it is impossible to prove that he was this person in a previous life. My client, however, believes that he was, and has been helped by this knowledge. And in the final analysis that is all that matters.

Do I Have a Soul Mate?

A soul mate is someone with whom you have had a powerful bond through many incarnations. Most people consider a soul mate relationship to be a strong love relationship between two people that has lasted for hundreds, maybe even thousands, of years. This frequently does occur, and it is always exciting for people to find that the person they adore in this lifetime was also their lover in previous incarnations.

Soul mate relationships can also include important relationships between two people that have nothing to do with love and romance. Someone who is your mentor in this lifetime, for example, may have been your teacher or student in a number of previous lifetimes. This can also be considered a soul mate relationship because it is strong, important, and vital to your progress even though it is platonic. Therefore, another benefit of returning to your past lives is that it enables you to determine exactly who your soul mates are.

2

Getting Ready

I find myself in some scene which I cannot have vis-
ited before and which is yet perfectly familiar; I
know that it was the stage of an action in which I
once took part and am about to take part in again.

John Buchan (1875–1940)

I believe that everybody can uncover memories of their past lives if they want to.
Unfortunately, in my clinical practice I've discovered that many people find it hard to let go
and allow themselves to relive a previous
incarnation. This can be the case even if they

desperately want to return to their past lives for a specific reason.

There are many possible reasons for this. A fear of letting go is the major one. This fear can be conscious or unconscious. Many people become sufficiently relaxed to drift back into their long-lost memories, only to pull back at the last moment.

Another common fear is that the person will uncover something terrifying or unbelievably tragic in a past life. Fortunately, a past-life regression can be terminated at any time and the person will safely return to the present. In my regression work I always tell my clients that they will experience their past lives in a slightly detached way. They can move closer, or step back, at any time.

Some people are skeptical about the whole process and do not allow it to happen. As long as they remain skeptical it is impossible for them to return to a previous lifetime. But if they temporarily suspend disbelief, they can surprise themselves with what can be accomplished.

In this book we will be discussing a dozen different methods of returning to your past lives. You may find it good to read the entire book and then experiment with the methods that appeal most to you. I have found that having a variety of methods to choose from is a good idea.

We all think and act in different ways. A method that quickly and easily transports me back to a past life may not be nearly as effective for you, and another method may work better for you than it will for me. Also, different methods seem to work better at different times. Read this book, choose a method that appeals to you, and practice it. You may find that it works extremely well, and in that case you may choose never to try the other methods. However, you might be like me and choose different methods depending on how you feel at any given time.

No matter which method you choose, have fun with it. This may sound strange, but you will experience better results if you conduct your regression with a sense of playfulness. Be serious about your need to learn about your past lives, but enjoy the process of discovering them. As with many other things in the psychic world, grim determination makes it almost impossible to achieve success.

Naturally, you will uncover unpleasant incidents in your past lives. Many of your past lives will be unhappy ones. People will have done hurtful things to you. Likewise, you will have harmed others at different times. You must realize that the person who received and gave this hurt is not the person you are now. If you stole, raped, or killed in your past lives, it doesn't mean that you're a terrible person in this lifetime. Revisiting past lives gives you an opportunity to forgive yourself for those past indiscretions. Past-life regressions also give you the opportunity to forgive others for what they did to you. You will derive enormous satisfaction from doing this.

You do not have to believe in reincarnation for these experiments to work. However, you must be serious and open-minded. You will have no success whatsoever if you treat the subject as a joke.

Naturally, you need to ensure that the room you are conducting the regression in is warm, and that you will not be disturbed. You may feel that lying in bed at night is the best place in which to return to a past life. In practice, this is not usually the case. Most people who try to do this—myself included—simply drift off to sleep. I find that a recliner chair in a warm room works well for me.

Many people like quiet meditative music in the background during regressions. Make sure that this music has no recognizable tunes as you want the music to help rather than distract you. I prefer a quiet room with no music, however, a musical background can help eliminate potentially distracting sounds. You should use it if you think it will help you relax.

It pays to have no expectations when you start. You may be convinced that you spent a lifetime in medieval

Barcelona and ask to be taken there. But the experiment is doomed to failure if, in fact, you have never lived there in any of your many lifetimes.

Some people are convinced that they were a famous person in the past. I have conducted regressions for hundreds of people over the years and have yet to meet the reincarnation of Henry VIII or Cleopatra. I would love to meet these people, but it has never happened. The chances are that you were an average person in your past life. In fact, I am always suspicious when someone tells me that they believe they were Napoleon or some other famous character from history. Although they may genuinely believe that this is the case, it is more likely that they are simply bolstering their self-esteem in this lifetime.

Once you have experienced and explored one of your past lives, examine other lifetimes. This will give you a much better picture of your soul's purpose than any single incarnation can. Each additional lifetime adds to the overall picture and provides further insights into the life that you are currently living.

After regressing yourself two or three times you may feel that you are simply making it all up and imagining your past lives. Many people feel this way. This is not surprising as your first regressions are likely to contain a variety of unconnected memories that may seem like total fantasies. However, as you practice the different methods and become more confident of your abilities of returning to your past lives, more and more valuable details will emerge.

After each regression allow some time to think about the experience before returning to your everyday life. See what lessons you had to learn. See what karmic factors were involved. In particular, see what karma is still affecting you in this lifetime. See what skills and talents you had in that previous lifetime. Forgive yourself for your past indiscretions. Forgive others for what they did to you. Realize that no matter what you were like in that past lifetime, you did the very best that you could. Remember that you are not the same person you were then. Consequently, there is no need for guilt or any recriminations. Finally, when you feel ready, stretch and get up.

Make notes of your experiences as soon as possible after the regression. These notes will become more and more valuable as time goes on.

Be careful when talking about your past-life experiments with others, at least in the early stages. Some people will not understand what you are doing and may even think that you have fallen into the clutches of satanic forces. I have experienced that myself and have even lost friends because of my explorations into the psychic world. Everyone is different and we are all at different stages in our development and progress. Be gentle and understanding when other people try to discourage you. Answer their questions, but do not try to force your ideas on anyone else.

Most people pursue their interest in past-life regression on their own, and so I wrote this book with a solitary practitioner in mind. However, there are many benefits to be obtained by working with a like-minded partner. A sympathetic and understanding partner can guide you through your regression and make the entire experience smoother and easier. Another advantage is that you can discuss each other's experiences afterward.

3

Karma

For every action, there is an equal and opposite reaction.

Sir Isaac Newton (1642–1727)

*K*arma is a Sanskrit word that is derived from the verb *kri,* meaning "to do" or "to activate." Consequently, *karma* literally means "a deed or activity." Karma describes the universal law of course and effect. Everything we think, say, or do creates a reaction or has an effect. In other words, we reap what we sow.

This is because the universe is a moral one, and eventually every deed, good or bad, will receive its due reward. If you do something bad today, you will ultimately receive something bad back as a consequence. It may not happen in this lifetime, but eventually you will have to pay for it. Likewise, a good deed done today means that you will be rewarded for it in the future. Good deeds and kindness shown to others in the present can help atone for bad karma created in the past. Consequently, although most people seem to associate karma with atoning for bad deeds, there is both good and bad karma.

Some people relate karma to predestination. This is not the case. Karma has nothing to do with fate or destiny. It is not a process of retribution or punishment. Karma is a process in which every action has a certain consequence. If you are faced with a moral choice and make the correct decision, you will gain good karma. If you choose to do the wrong thing, you will ultimately have to pay the price. It is as simple as that. I have given many talks in prisons and have met numerous people there who are paying the price for making the wrong choice. However, these are only the people who got caught. Many criminals appear to get away with making the wrong choice. At least, that is what it looks like. But sooner or later, in this lifetime or the next, they will undoubtedly pay for whatever it is they did.

The concept of karma may sound like a process of reward and punishment. In fact, it is much more than that. Karma gives us opportunities to grow. It provides us with obstacles and opportunities. The life you are living now is the direct result of everything you have ever done in your previous lives. In this lifetime you will be presented with challenges, difficulties, and opportunities. The way in which you handle these will dictate what your next life will be like. No one is ever given more than they can handle.

In his book *Karma and Rebirth*, Christmas Humphreys described karma in this way: "Man is punished by his sins, not for them. Karma neither rewards nor punishes; it only restores lost harmony. He who suffers, deserves his suffering, and he who has reason to rejoice is reaping where he has sown."[1]

People who are aware of the concept of karma are in a much better position to progress positively than people who know nothing about it and are leading their lives in a haphazard, undirected manner. Even more important than this is the fact that people who actively seek to work out their karma appear to receive protection and help from divine forces. This is because they are working in accordance with God's will rather than fighting against it. It does not release them from their karmic debts, but it does strengthen them and enable them to move forward in a more positive and directed manner.

One of the most powerful ways of releasing karma is to forgive others and yourself. If someone wrongs you and you are compassionate and forgive them unreservedly, you will build up good karma. Interestingly, forgiving others also sends out messages to the universe that encourages others to forgive you. We all make mistakes as we go through life, and it is important to forgive yourself also.

Interestingly, there are many references to karma in the Bible. In Job 4:8 we read, "Even as I have seen, they that plow iniquity, and sow wickedness, reap the same." In Revelation 2:23 we read, ". . . I will give unto every one of you according to your works." The most famous reference is found in Galatians 6:7: "God is not mocked; for whatsoever a man soweth that shall he also reap." Jesus made an indirect reference to the karma created by thought in his Sermon on the Mount: "Ye have heard that it was said by them of old time, Thou shalt not commit adultery: But I say unto you, That whosoever looketh on a woman to lust after her hath committed adultery with her already in his heart" (Matthew 5:27–28).[2]

Over the last twenty years a great deal of research has been done on near-death experiences. One of the most astounding discoveries is that the experiences most people reported on returning to life are virtually identical to those recorded in the *Tibetan Book of the Dead*. This appears to indicate that these people ventured at least a short way into *bardo,* the state of consciousness that we experience in between lives. Dr. Joel Whitton, a Toronto neuropsychiatrist, was one of the first to research this subject and found that many people work out a type of "karmic script" while waiting to be reborn. While in the bardo state they choose the type of career they will undertake in their next life, the type of marriage partner they will have, parents, and so on.[3] This enables these people to arrange experiences that will allow them to work on karma from previous lifetimes. Of course, whether or not they succeed in this is a different matter.

Our motives play an important role in karma. If, for example, a wealthy person builds a hospital as a gift for the community, he will unquestionably gain karmic benefit for his generosity. However, the degree of benefit is determined by his motives. If the building is donated because of a desire to help people, the karmic benefits will be large. If he makes the gift with other motives, such as bolstering his ego or helping his political aspirations, the benefits will be much less.

There is equilibrium in the universe, and whatever we do, sooner or later it will be balanced to restore that state of equilibrium. More than one hundred years ago Ralph Waldo Emerson expressed this concept extremely well when he wrote, "If you love and serve men, you cannot by any hiding or stratagem escape the remuneration. Secret retributions are always restoring the level, when disturbed, of the divine justice. It is impossible to tilt the beam. All the tyrants and proprietors and monopolists of the world in vain set their shoulders to heave the bar. Settles for evermore the ponderous equator to its line, and man and mote, and star and sun must range to it, or be pulverized by the recoil."[4]

Carl Jung came to no decision as to whether or not the karma he carried came solely from this life or from all of his lives. However, he had a good approach to the subject. In his autobiography he wrote, "When I die, my deeds will follow along with me—that is how I imagine it. I will bring with me what I have done. In the meantime it is important to ensure that I do not stand at the end with empty hands."[5] In other words, we all need to do the very best we can in this lifetime.

Karma is one of the oldest doctrines in the world. The fact that it is still accepted by more than half of the world's population is due to its basic impartial fairness. As you sow, so shall you reap.

4

Dreaming of Your Past Lives

All that we see or seem
Is but a dream within a dream.

Edgar Allan Poe (1809–1849)

My students look at me in horror whenever I suggest that they can recapture and relive their past lives in their dreams. "We don't remember our dreams," they say. "How can we remember our past lives by dreaming about them?" Fortunately, you can learn to remember your dreams, and you can also direct your dreams so that they will reveal valuable information about your past lives.

Dreams are the thoughts, sensations, images, and emotions that pass through our minds while we are asleep. They are part of an altered state of consciousness which we enter into every night. On average about 20 percent of our sleep is spent in a dream state. For most people, this is about an hour and a half every night.[1]

Dreaming is an essential part of our lives. We have between four to seven dreams every night. On average we spend between six and seven years of our lives dreaming. In fact, if we failed to dream we would become very ill. Research has shown that people suffering from depression have fewer dreams than usual. When they start dreaming more, as shown by an increase in rapid eye movement, it is a sign that they are getting well again.[2]

Dreams have fascinated people since time began. Dream research has been going on for a long while too. The first serious book on the subject was by Marquis d'Hervey de Saint-Denys who tried to influence his own dreams. He even played music at night in an attempt to stimulate certain types of dreams. His book *Dreams and How to Guide Them* appeared in 1867.[3]

Unfortunately, it was not widely distributed. Even Sigmund Freud was never able to locate a copy.

A significant breakthrough occurred in 1953 when researchers discovered that rapid eye movements during sleep indicated that a person was dreaming. In their early experiments, researchers found that twenty out of twenty-seven people reported vivid dreams when awakened while rapid eye movements were in progress. However, only four people out of twenty-three remembered their dreams when awakened at a time when they were not making rapid eye movements.[4]

Many thousands of experiments have been conducted since then. On average, 80 percent of people awakened during REM (rapid eye movement) sleep reported highly visual dreams. People awakened at other times also report dreams 30 to 50 percent of the time, but they are not as visual and appear more like thoughts.

When you wake up normally after a night's sleep, the chances are high that you will have a vague recollection of a dream. However, once you get up and begin your day, this memory will quickly disappear.

A dream diary is an extremely useful tool for capturing your dreams. If possible, lie in bed for a few minutes after waking and think about the dream. Move as little as possible. For some unknown reason, dream recall appears to be easier if you think about your dream while in the same position you were in while dreaming it. As you do this, more and more information will come to you as you gradually recall the dream. Be gentle with yourself. Do not try to force vague impressions to become clearer. Focus on the elements that you can recall and see what else appears.

Then when you feel ready, record everything that you can remember. I use a dream diary that I keep beside the bed. You may prefer to record your impressions onto cassette, or even draw a picture of your memories. The method you use is not important, just as long as you find it easy to do and helpful when you are reviewing your dreams at a later date.

Many of my students have found it helpful to start by writing down a few key words or phrases. They found that writing down a few words helped clarify the dream in their minds, thereby making it easier for them to then write out the entire dream.

It is important that you write down everything you can remember. Do not elaborate or censor anything. You might be surprised or shocked with what comes to the surface. It does not matter. Write it down exactly as you remember it. Many times dreams are not complete in themselves but gradually unfold over a period of time. If you censor unclear details from your dream diary, you will lose important information that may become clear later on. Obviously, you will need to keep your dream diary in a safe place. Keep it locked away if necessary.

Naturally, none of this will work if you wake up in a panic and have to leap out of bed to go to work. In a case like this you might have to set your alarm clock to go off ten minutes earlier than usual. This will give you enough time to think about your dreams and write them down. Alternatively, you might focus on remembering your dreams during the weekend or at any other time when you do not need an alarm clock to wake you.

Another method is to dictate your dreams to someone whom you implicitly trust. This is what Joan Grant, the famous author, did. She found that many of her dreams were about her life in previous incarnations. She trained herself to wake up several times each night and write down what she had been dreaming about. The more she did this, the more involved the dreams became, and eventually her husband wrote them down for her. However, he became extremely concerned when she decided to seek publication of them, as he did not want anyone to learn about his wife's belief in reincarnation. Joan Grant's first book,

Winged Pharaoh, appeared in 1937 and became a best-seller. Not surprisingly, it also marked the end of her first marriage. Although no one knew it at the time, *Winged Pharaoh* was the story of one of her past lives. Ultimately she wrote seven historical novels that were actually accounts of her previous lifetimes.[4]

There are other things you can do to enhance your dream recall. It is easier to remember your dreams in the morning if you have had a good night's sleep. If you go to bed extremely late or immediately after eating a large meal, the chances are that you will not recall your dreams. The same thing applies if you go to bed after overindulging in alcohol or drugs. You are much more likely to remember your dreams if you go to bed in a peaceful, relaxed state of mind.

As you drift off to sleep, tell yourself that you will remember your dreams when you wake up. Something as simple as this can make a big difference in the number of dreams you recall in the morning. This is because we are much more likely to remember something that is important to us than something that is of little account. If you take your dreams seriously, your ability to remember them will improve rapidly.

Everyone I know who has tried this has increased their ability to remember their dreams. Instead of remembering vague impressions that quickly fade, they gain vivid details and a much clearer picture of what is going on. This is not surprising as they have taken a positive, active role in remembering their dreams once they wake up.

If you wake up in the morning with no memories of any dreams, lie quietly for a few minutes with your eyes closed. Think about your need to remember your dreams and see what comes back to you. Sometimes a forgotten dream will come back into your mind while you are lying quietly in bed waiting for it to return. It is important to simply allow this to happen. You are doomed to failure if you try to force a dream back into your conscious awareness. Dreams are elusive and do not respond to pressure. It is wonderful if a dream does return in this way, but do not worry if nothing comes back. Simply get up when you feel ready and start your day. Remain confident that you will remember your dreams on the following morning.

Experiment with this for two weeks before attempting a dream that gives insight into one of your past lifetimes. You will find the experience rewarding, insightful, and endlessly fascinating.

The late D. Scott Rogo wrote a book on past lives called *The Search for Yesterday: A Critical Examination of the Evidence for Reincarnation.* In the course of his research he placed advertisements in magazines asking to hear from people who had experienced past-life recall without using a regression technique. He found that in the majority of credible instances, these people had revisited their past lives while dreaming.

Once you have gained expertise at recalling your dreams, you can move on to experience dreams that relate to your many past lives. This is easier than you might imagine.

When you go to bed, tell yourself that tonight you will have a dream about one of your past lives and that you will remember it when you wake up. Think about your desire to recall your past lives, and then tell yourself again that you will have a dream about a past life and will remember it in the morning.

If you had success with the earlier experiment about recalling your dreams, you will find a variety of impressions in your mind when you wake up after this experiment. Do not try to analyze them right away. Allow them to flow into your conscious mind and form a picture or impression. If you lie quietly and allow this process to continue, all sorts of other insights will come into your mind. Then as soon as possible record everything that you can remember.

It is possible that you will wake up with no memory of the dreams you had. This is unlikely if you have become proficient at recalling your dreams. However, it can happen. Do not worry when this occurs. Try again the following night, and the night after if need be. If you keep practicing in a positive state of mind, the memories of your past lives will come back to you.

Analyzing the Results

It may take several nights for a complete picture to come to you. This is why it is important to record everything that you can remember, even if it does not appear to fit in with the rest of the information you gained. Sometimes the same information will be given to you several nights in a row. Examination of this will usually provide greater detail every time.

Some years ago I was talking about reincarnation dreams on a radio program. A few weeks later I was contacted by a couple who had tried the technique and found that it worked. They were thrilled with their success but were puzzled by something. Gladys, the wife, learned everything about her past life in a storybook form, almost as if she was watching a film. On the other hand, Bill, her husband, received tantalizing glimpses of different scenes that did not make any sense until several nights had passed. It seemed unfair, they told me, that one received the entire past life whole in a single dream, while the other learned it all piecemeal.

The answer is that we all have different ways of thinking, and consequently our methods of recall are different too. I could understand Bill's frustration as it took him several nights to gain the same amount of information that Gladys had learned in one. And her recall came back fully formed and complete, while he had to gradually sort out and arrange his. However, in the long run it does not matter how much time it takes to gain back your long-lost memories, just as long as they do return.

Bill's recall was interesting for a number of reasons. After the first night he woke up trembling with a strong impression of a bayonet and a German military helmet. He had no idea if he was a German soldier or if a German soldier was attacking him. He thought possibly the latter as he woke up full of fear.

The following morning provided no new clues about that. He remembered a quiet domestic scene. He, his wife, and two young children were enjoying breakfast in a courtyard setting overlooking a wide, gently flowing river. There was a large castle on the opposite side of the river. Bill thought that it must be the Rhine River.

In his dream on the third night, Bill was standing at a counter and people were coming up and abusing him. There seemed to be nothing he could do to stop it so he broke down and cried. He thought he saw the bayonet again, but was not sure.

On the fourth night Bill saw himself at a funeral. His wife and daughter were standing beside him. He realized that he was attending the funeral of his young son. After the funeral the family walked home and he saw himself in a mirror. He was wearing a military uniform and realized that he was an officer in the German army. On the next morning Bill woke up with no clear pictures in his mind but with the realization that his wife in his previous life was his daughter in this lifetime.

The following night's dream brought back a memory of a tactical meeting with Kaiser Wilhelm. There were several other officers in the room and Bill realized that he was a senior officer in the German army. He woke with a horrible feeling of forboding as he knew the war had been lost.

On the seventh morning Bill woke with a clear memory of lying in a hospital waiting to die. His wife and grown-up daughter were sitting beside him. His daughter was heavily pregnant. He wanted to speak to them to say how much he loved them, but the words would not come. He cried tears of frustration which his wife tenderly wiped away. He lay in bed watching them, and as he watched the picture gradually faded. Suddenly all he could see was blackness, and he realized that he had died.

Bill was able to put these different memories into perspective only after the final dream. "I was a sensitive, caring man who hated war but became successful because of it," he told me. "I had a love of beauty, and am convinced that I was a dealer in works of art in that lifetime. I didn't want to fight, but became involved against my will. I benefited financially because the contacts I made during the war became my clients afterwards. Was it a happy life? It's hard to say. There were moments when I felt proud and fulfilled, but much of the time I was ashamed of what I was doing."

I asked him if he felt proud and fulfilled in his current life. He stroked his jaw as he pondered this. "I've never really thought about it before," he said. "But I think the answer must be 'yes.' I have strong moral values, and I haven't done anything that I'm really ashamed of. I remember as a teenager walking away from my friends when they were about to do something I thought was wrong." He smiled. "Maybe I did learn something from that past life after all. I did all sorts of things that I shouldn't have. I could justify it by saying it was wartime, and I had no choice, but is that really the case?"

Gladys's past life was much simpler. She was the only daughter of a wealthy English family living in southeast

England in the eighteenth century. She was doted on by her parents and married the older son of her parent's best friends. It was a happy marriage and they had seven children. She outlived them all and saw herself on her deathbed surrounded by grandchildren, all of whom loved her. "It was certainly a happy life," she told me. "Uneventful, boring even, but I was always surrounded by love."

"How does that fit in with this life?"

Gladys looked at her husband. "Bill and I have discussed this quite a bit. I think in my past life I was self-centered and gave no thought to people less fortunate than myself. In this life I am still fortunate in my friends and family, but I devote a large proportion of my time to charitable work." She squeezed Bill's hand. "Maybe too much time." Even though Gladys and Bill learned about their past lives in different ways, they both found them helpful in answering questions in this lifetime.

Gladys and Bill also had a desire to explore these past lives further. There are two ways of doing this using dreamwork. One is to carry on the way they began. When they go to sleep at night they need to tell themselves that they will return to this specific past life to learn more about it. The other method is to explore their past lives with lucid dreaming. (There is also a third method which we will discuss later in this chapter.)

Lucid Dreaming

A lucid dream is a dream in which you are aware that you are dreaming. Most people have experienced the sensation of becoming aware that they are dreaming, but the dream usually takes over and the conscious mind returns to sleep. Yet it is possible in this situation to deliberately allow the conscious mind to direct the dream. Once you are in control of the dream, you can take it wherever you wish.

Edgar Cayce experienced an extraordinary lucid dream during World War I. Edgar's wife Gertrude gave birth to a son, their second, in 1910. Sadly, the baby lived for only two months. Some years later Edgar dreamed that he had met and talked with some of his Sunday school pupils who had been killed during the war. While in the dream, Edgar thought that if he had been able to see these young soldiers, even though they were dead, there must be a way in which he could see his son. Instantly he found himself amongst tiers of babies, one of whom was his son, smiling. This dream consoled the grieving father who was then able to move forward in his own life.[5] This is a striking example of just how useful lucid dreaming can be.

There are a number of things you can do that will increase the chances of lucid dreaming.

Step One—Preparation

Before falling asleep tell yourself that you will experience a lucid dream. It is important that you tell yourself this in a casual, almost offhand, way. You might say to yourself, "Tonight, as I dream, I will realize that I am dreaming and I will dream of [*whatever you want to experience*]." If you insist that you will have a lucid dream, the chances are that you will not have one.

Decide on a certain action you will take in the lucid dream. This could be anything at all. Keep it simple to begin with. Later on you might decide to visit a friend or relative.

Step Two—Enter into a Lucid Dream

If you wake up during the night and feel that you are dropping straight back into sleep, tell yourself that you will experience a lucid dream.

If you frequently dream of a certain object or event, tell yourself that the next time this situation occurs you will immediately become aware of your conscious mind and will be able to experience a lucid dream.

Experiencing a lucid dream is one of the most exciting things you will ever do. There is no limit to where you can travel or what you can do. For instance, you can move back and forth in time, visit other planets, or check up on relatives living in other parts of the world. You can also explore your past lives in more detail than any other method.

Step Three—Return to a Past Life

Once you become aware that you are lucid dreaming, tell yourself to return to one of your past lives and see where the experience takes you. (Naturally, if you are familiar with some of your previous incarnations, you can return to one of them if you wish.)

You can move back and forth in time in this past life just as you can mentally in this current lifetime. While experiencing that past life, see if you can find out what your main purpose was in that lifetime. See what you enjoyed doing, who was important to you, what you did for a living, and anything else that occurs to you.

The advantage of lucid dreaming is that you can become as close as you wish to any event or experience. If something seems painful or emotional, you can observe it from a distance. You can even move away completely if you desire. Likewise, you can move closer and closer to joyful, happy occasions and experience them again just as you did the first time.

Step Four—Return to the Present

You are always aware that you are lucid dreaming and can return to the present whenever you wish. Unfortunately, you will sometimes find yourself back in the present long before you are ready to return. Often if an event seems painful, dangerous, overly emotional, or traumatic, you will appear to be jerked back into the present. This is your survival instinct working to protect you. Sometimes it will happen when you least expect it, and this can be annoying.

Remain calm when this happens. Lie quietly in bed and see if you can return to your past life. Often you will feel yourself returning to your lucid dream, and you can carry on with your exploration. I find the best way to do this is to think about the setting of that past life. By thinking about the buildings, trees, and other objects in the environment, I frequently drift back into the same dream and can carry on from where I left off.

At other times you will simply return to sleep. There is nothing that can be done about this. Enjoy your sleep and remain confident that you will remember your lucid dream when you wake up.

Step Five—Record Your Lucid Dream

Make notes about the experience when you wake up in the morning, and return to that past life on the following night. By doing this you will gradually build up a complete record of your many past lives.

Lucid dreaming takes practice. I believe that everyone can learn to do it, but even skilled practitioners find it hard to lucid dream on demand. Fortunately, there is also conscious dreaming.

Conscious Dreaming

Conscious dreaming is similar to lucid dreaming. In fact, a conscious dream frequently turns into a lucid dream. In a lucid dream you become aware that you are dreaming and then proceed to direct the dream. In conscious dreaming you are awake and direct your thoughts toward whatever your purpose may be.

Go to bed at your usual time, close your eyes, and relax. It is important that you are not overtired and have not consumed too much food and drink. Think about your desire to explore one of your past lives. Allow different thoughts to flow through your mind. Avoid any negative thoughts. If you find yourself thinking along those lines, simply let them go. Tell yourself that you'll worry about them tomorrow and have better things to do now.

When you feel completely relaxed, think about different events that have happened in your life and visualize your surroundings as they occurred. You might choose events when you were away from home and the surroundings were more exotic than usual. I invariably think about my visit to the Temple of Poseidon at Sounion near Athens whenever I do this exercise. It does not matter what events you think about, as long as they are positive ones and you can visualize the surroundings. Go back as far in your life as you possibly can. If you return all the way to early childhood and nothing triggers a response in your mind, stop concentrating on your surroundings and instead focus on the faces, sounds, and feelings that pop into your mind.

You may find that one particular scene captures your attention more than the others. If this occurs, focus on it and see where it takes you. You may find that it transports you into a lucid dream that relates to a past life. If it does not appear to lead anywhere, let it go and return to the present. Sometimes conscious dreaming of this sort meanders for a while and then, quite suddenly, you will be literally sucked into a lucid dream of one of your previous lifetimes.

Frequently you will drift off to sleep before this conscious dreaming leads you into a lucid dream. When you wake up in the morning, however, you will probably have a strong recall of events that took place in a past life.

Another method you may prefer to try is a form of Tibetan dream yoga that encourages conscious dreaming. Lie down on your side with your knees slightly bent. Close your eyes and think of your purpose in entering a dream state. Visualize a beautiful, vibrantly blue lotus flower inside your throat. Imagine it slowly opening and observe an incredibly pure white light emerging from its center. Feel this white light gradually fill and surround you with protection, peace, and serenity. As the lotus slowly opens, hear the mantric word *Om* [aum] repeated over and over again in your mind.

Simply remain aware of the beautiful lotus flower, the white light, and the mantric sound. Breathe slowly and deeply and remain expectantly aware. Soon you will become aware that you are dreaming, even though you are still awake. Go with the dream and see where it takes you. If necessary, guide it gently toward one of your past lives.[6]

Conscious Daydreaming

A form of conscious dreaming can also be done while you are awake. This is the third method that I alluded to earlier. It is a form of daydreaming.

Step One—Preparation

You will need at least half an hour, preferably longer, for this exercise. Sit down quietly where you won't be disturbed, close your eyes, and take a few deep breaths.

Step Two—Think About Your Past-Life Memories

Think about the past-life memories that have come to you in your dreams. Take your time with this. Experience these memories as completely and as vividly as possible.

Step Three—Ask for Further Insight

Once you have done step two, see if you can uncover further memories of this past life. There is no need to strain for results; remain relaxed. Daydream and see what comes into your mind. Often you will be able to carry on from where your dream left off. Take the memories as far as you can.

Step Four—Return to the Present

Stop the exercise when you feel that you have learned all that you can in this session, or when the daydream starts moving into areas that are not related to your past life. The gentlest way to return to full conscious awareness is to take five deep breaths before opening your eyes.

Step Five—Record Your Findings

Write down everything you can remember as soon as possible after finishing the exercise. Most people tend to think that they will remember everything that happened during one of these sessions. Unfortunately, the memories often fade quickly.

Learning to direct and recall your dreams is a highly effective way of recovering long-lost memories of previous lifetimes. Some people find it easy to recall their past lives in this way, while others need to persist to achieve satisfactory results. But dream work is valuable for many purposes in addition to recovering past lives. It can aid in self-understanding, provide glimpses of the future, allow you to receive hunches and warnings, and let you become totally in control of your life. Julius Caesar was well aware of this; he crossed the Rubicon because of a dream. Any effort you put into remembering your dreams will prove worthwhile.

Joanna's Experience

Joanna came to my classes in search of a solution to the troubling dreams she was having. Joanna was fifty-two and had been married twice. Her first marriage was disastrous, and her second husband had died while out on a fishing trip several years before I met her.

"I think I got over Frank's death very well," she told me on our first meeting. "We were very close, and it was devastating, but as they say, time is a great healer, and life goes on."

Joanna and Frank had owned a small distributing business, and after his death she put all her energies into the business. It had grown and a year ago she had sold it for a large amount of money.

"I'm free to do anything I want," she told me. "The only problem is I've no idea what I want."

Then she told me about her dreams. For the previous three months she had woken up in the middle of every night gagging. "It's as if someone is trying to strangle me, and I open my eyes and see this terrifying brown face staring at me. His eyes are full of hate and menace. After that I get up as it's impossible to get to sleep again."

"Do you recognize the face?" I asked.

Joanna shook her head. "It's familiar," she said. "Very familiar, but I can't recognize it. It's a mystery."

It sounded as if Joanna was experiencing a partial recall of a past life. This is the sort of information that would return involuntarily if Joanna had been strangled in a previous lifetime. Traumatic experiences create a profound effect upon the mind. This is why so many people recall dying in a previous lifetime.

I suggested to Joanna that she try to direct the dream rather than waking up. In other words, I was suggesting that she turn it into a lucid dream. Although Joanna was experiencing the same dream every night, the experience was so terrifying that it took her several weeks to gain control of it. Once she succeeded she could hardly wait to tell me about it.

"I did what you suggested," Joanna said. "I told myself that I was dreaming and could follow the dream backwards or forwards. I went backwards first. My husband's name was Gerard, but he was Frank, if you know what I mean. He and I had a small farm. We had created it out of nothing, and although it was very modest, we felt proud of it. I was pregnant and having a hard time of it, but Gerard never complained. Life was difficult, but we knew it would get better once we had a family to help.

"We had neighbors a mile down the road. I liked Millie but couldn't stand her husband, Joel. The way he looked at me gave me the creeps. You could tell he was undressing me in his mind."

Gerard and Joel used to go to town together to get provisions. It took them three days. I remember having a strange feeling of forboding one spring morning when they set off. Joel was almost slobbering as he stared at me, and I was pleased to see them go. But then I started worrying. That was nothing new. I always worried when Gerard was away, and now, five months gone, I was more worried than usual. I slept badly the first night. The next night I was so tired I went straight to sleep. It was the smell of alcohol that woke me. Then I felt strong hands on my neck. I opened my eyes and started to move; Joel was on top of me. I yelled out and struggled to get free. It was a waste of time shouting as no one could hear, but I couldn't move with him on top of me, his hands going everywhere. I managed to bite him. I can still taste his blood. That annoyed him and he hit me again and again. And then he strangled me."

Joanna half smiled as she finished her story. "It didn't all come out in one night," she explained. "It was too horrific. But bit by bit I got the whole story."

"Are you still having that dream?" I asked.

Joanna shook her head. "It seems to have gone, but I know how to handle it now. I move the dream forward into the future. I see two wooden graves side by side. Gerard and me."

"What about Joel?"

Joanna shook her head. "I don't know what happened to him. I'll find out one day." She laughed. "One thing I do know is that Frank and I were together before, and we'll be together again in the future. I have no doubts about that whatsoever."

5

Far Memory

Our birth is but a sleep and a forgetting;
The soul that rises with us, our life's star,
  Hath had elsewhere its setting,
    And cometh from afar.
    Not in entire forgetfulness
    And not in utter nakedness
But trailing clouds of glory do we come
  From God who is our home.

William Wordsworth (1770–1850)

More than twenty years ago a good friend told me about this method of recapturing past lives. Stephen was in his eighties and was suffering from insomnia. He would go to bed feeling tired, but hours later would still be tossing and turning, totally unable to drift into sleep.

To help fill in these sleepless hours Stephen began going back through his life, remembering as much as he could. Eventually he got back to his early childhood in the east end of London and saw himself out shopping with his mother. He found that, with practice, he was able to recall the name of every shop on the street. Stephen was delighted to discover that his memory was just about perfect and that he could easily see the street and all the shops in his mind's eye.

One night Stephen tried to go back even further. He found himself as a crying baby in his mother's arms. She was running, and instinctively Stephen knew that she was taking him to the hospital. Apparently he almost died and would have if his mother had not rushed him to the hospital. Despite being no more than one year old, Stephen had had a near-death experience.

"I don't remember it consciously," he told me. "But when I went back over the experience in my mind, it was so strong. I almost died and it was entirely due to my mother that I survived. No wonder Mum always called me the 'miracle boy.'"

Stephen was fascinated to discover that he could remember events that happened when he was only one year old. He returned to that incident again and again. Eventually, he decided to see if he could go back even further.

"I felt a warmness and a feeling of peace and comfort," he said. "I thought that perhaps I'd returned to the womb. But then suddenly I was an adult and I experienced terror." Stephen's eyes widened as he told me the story. "I was so shocked that I returned to the present. My bed was drenched with sweat and my heart was pumping as if I'd run a steeplechase."

Despite his feelings of terror, Stephen felt drawn back to the scene. A night or two later he took himself back to his time in the womb, and then, suddenly, he found himself a young man again, dressed in rags and hiding in a swamp while men and dogs searched for him.

"My mouth was dry and my heart was racing. I could hear the dogs getting closer and closer but I was exhausted. I'd run and run and could run no more. The smell of the swamp was overpowering, but I lay down as the dogs came running along the bank. I was sure they'd found me but they kept on going, and soon it became quiet. I was uncomfortable and my stomach began rumbling, but I stayed there in the swamp until it was dark. When I got up it was cold and I was wet and caked in mud and filth.

"I didn't know what to do. I went into the woods and sat under a tree, listening to the sounds of the night while the coldness slowly crept up my body. I waited, knowing what was going to happen. I think I smiled as my spirit left my body."

Stephen had shown no previous interest in reincarnation and was only mildly interested in the possibility that he had lived before. However, he became obsessed with the young man whose last day of life he remembered so vividly. He now looked forward to going to bed, because each night he learned a little bit more about the person he had been in his previous lifetime. He filled notebooks with everything he could remember, and planned to write a book about his earlier life. Stephen phoned me with great excitement one day to tell me that he had bought a computer so that he could write his book. Sadly, he died just a few weeks later, leaving behind dozens of notebooks that are next to impossible to read.

Stephen gradually became convinced that he was recalling a past life. He found the entire concept of reincarnation disturbing, as he thought that "once is enough for anyone." We used to have fascinating discussions on the subject, and I continually encouraged him to go back even further and see how many previous lifetimes he could remember. Stephen never did this as he became so fascinated with the lifetime he had uncovered.

Stephen's experiment, intended originally to fill in his sleepless hours, taught me that we remember much more than we think we do.

Far Memory Technique

Far memory is a deceptively easy technique that many people use to learn about their past lives. Although the technique sounds like simplicity itself, it takes practice to achieve success. My friend Stephen spent many months recalling incidents in his present life before accidentally returning to an earlier lifetime. Consequently, it is a good idea to have several sessions to see how far back you can return in this lifetime before moving back into another life.

Step One—Get Comfortable

Make yourself comfortable. It does not matter where you do this, just as long as you are comfortable and warm. In the summer months I enjoy experimenting with far memory outdoors. Usually, though, I lie down on a bed or sit in a comfortable chair. It does not matter where you choose, but it is important that you will not be disturbed. Many people prefer to do this experiment in bed at night.

Step Two—Take Deep Breaths

Close your eyes and take several deep breaths, breathing slowly and deeply. Breathe in as you silently count up to five, hold the breath for another count of five, and exhale to the count of eight.

Step Three—Relax

Relax as much as you possibly can. You might find it helpful to repeat to yourself, "I am completely relaxed. I am completely relaxed."

Step Four—Visualize an Important Scene from the Recent Past

Visualize an important event in your life that happened over the last few years. People see things in different ways. If you are a visual person you will see the event clearly in your mind. But it is just as valid if you hear or feel or sense the experience. This simply means that you are an auditory or kinesthetic person, and you experience a given event in your own particular way.

Because they are so intense, smells are an extremely effective way of returning to past lives. It is amazing how different scents bring back such powerful memories. Of the six senses, only smell goes first to the limbic system which is the part of the brain that seems to be involved with memory, emotion, and self-preservation.

Step Five—Visualize an Earlier Scene

Once you have the important event clear in your mind, let go of it and allow yourself to drift back to an event that happened much earlier in your life. It makes no difference how old you were when this event transpired, just as long as you are moving back in time.

Step Six—Repeat Step Five Several Times

Once you have successfully visualized the event, let it go, and drift even further back. Keep doing this until you have gone back as far as it is possible for you to go in this lifetime. It makes no difference if you are ten months, ten years, or twenty years old.

Step Seven—Go Back as Far as You Can

Now that you have gone back as far as you can, think of your desire to return to one of your past lives and then see if you can go back any further. There are three possibilities now: you may return to an even earlier experience in your current life, you may find yourself in a past life, or nothing at all will happen.

Step Eight—Explore Your Past Life

If you have returned to an earlier event in your current life, repeat step seven as many times as are necessary until you find yourself in a past life. When you find yourself in a past life, make yourself familiar with the scene you find yourself within and explore it. If nothing happens and you fail to go back to a past life or an earlier scene in your present life, simply return to the present and repeat the exercise again at a later date. Few people succeed on their first attempt, and you may have to repeat this exercise many times until you suddenly find yourself in a past life. That is why this is a good exercise to do in bed at night. If you fail to return to a previous lifetime, you are relaxed and can simply drift off to sleep. And if you return to a past life, you can explore it for as long as you wish and then fall asleep.

Step Nine—Return to This Past Life Whenever You Wish

Once you have recovered memories of your past life, no matter how fragmented they are, you will have no difficulty returning to that past life in the future to learn more. Once the door has been opened, you will be able to return to it as often as you wish.

Rather than focusing on important events that have happened, you can start with any event that happened to you yesterday. Once this is clear in your mind, think of something that happened last week. See if you can think of something that occurred a week earlier, followed by last month, and so on. The idea is to think of as many incidents as you can while moving steadily backward through time.

The far memory method sounds easy and it is for some people. However, I have known people who practiced this method for months on end without success. The most important factor is to simply relax and allow it to happen. Most people become frustrated when they do not get immediate results. Nothing worthwhile happens without a great deal of hard work and effort. You are most likely to be successful if you practice this exercise in an almost carefree manner.

Kirsty's Experience

Kirsty is in her middle forties. She married young and was divorced with two children by the time she was twenty-three. She brought up her daughters on her own and remarried two years ago. Today Kirsty runs the office in her husband's business. She is happier than she has ever been.

"Part of that is because I've uncovered several of my past lives," she told me. "Discovering that this lifetime is not all there is was very encouraging for me. I've been able to see the times when I've progressed, and the times when I slipped back. I've also located a number of karmic factors that I'm working on."

Kirsty's preferred method of returning to a past life is far memory. "I like the technique," she explained. "It appeals to my logical mind, and quite incidentally, it seems to have improved my memory. I seem to know so much more about this lifetime than I used to.

"I always do the far memory exercise in bed at night. I'm too busy the rest of the time. I only do it if I'm not too tired, as otherwise I fall asleep before I get there."

Kirsty's first regression was an unforgettable experience for her. "I'd always called my first husband a bastard for ruining our marriage. If it hadn't been for his drinking and drugs we'd probably still be together. As time went by I gradually began to understand what it must have been like for him. He had a small business that went bad, and I was so busy with the children that I didn't give him the help or support he needed. All the same, I kept on calling him names for years, and went out of my way to make it hard for him to see the girls. I blamed him for everything, but of course, there are two sides to every story. Recently I discovered that he never blamed me for anything. In fact, no matter what I did, he always spoke well of me.

"Well, when I first went back to a past life, I found I was a man. Not a very good one, either. I was a gambler and made my living by my wits. People had tried to kill me, so I guess I cheated to make a living.

"Anyway, I had a wife who loved me to bits. She was beautiful and I was so proud of her. Funnily enough, she is Jeremy [her first husband] in this lifetime. It was for her that I tried to go straight and lead an honest life. Of course, it didn't work. As soon as times got tough, I'd be back cheating others.

"My wife warned me several times that if I kept doing that she'd leave and go home to her parents. Finally, she did. I went away for a couple of months. Gambling on the riverboats. When I came back home with my pockets full of money, she wasn't there. Just a note saying she couldn't take it anymore.

"I went to her folks' home but they wouldn't tell me where she was. I told them I was changing my ways and gave them my address. They promised to give it to her, and I've no idea if they ever did 'cause I never saw her again. I died in a drunken fight outside a bar. I was forty-two years old."

Kirsty was visibly upset after telling me this. When she was ready, I asked her how this past life had relevance to her present life.

"He left me in that lifetime. I left him in this one."

"So in a sense, you paid him back for leaving you last time?"

Kirsty shook her head. "No, I don't think so. He had to leave me last time, as I was a criminal. It was no life for him. This time round, I had to leave him, because of the alcohol and drugs and abuse. Someone would have been killed if we'd stayed together. But don't you see, we're important to each other. Maybe we're soul mates in a strange sort of way, even though we haven't been able to make it work so far. I think we'll have another relationship next time around, and I hope it will work out better than before."

"What about your present husband?"

Kirsty smiled. "He's a wonderful man. I couldn't ask for anyone better. He's kind, understanding, considerate, and loving. But I don't think there's a karmic link there. This may sound funny, but I look at him as my reward for good behavior! He thinks I'm crazy looking into my past lives, but he's never made fun of it. I couldn't have a more supportive husband."

6

Past-Life Regressions

Because it is sometimes so unbelievable, the truth escapes becoming known.

Heraclitus (540?–460 B.C.E.)

When most people think of being regressed back to a past life, they think of hypnosis. Unfortunately, the word *hypnosis* scares many people. They have a mental picture of being brainwashed or losing control. Some think that the hypnotist will ask them to do something embarrassing.

None of these things are possible. When you are hypnotized you are more aware than you are normally. You know exactly what is going on. If, for instance, you go back to a lifetime at the court of Henry VIII, you would be at Hampton Court, but at the same time you would be aware that you were in the hypnotherapist's office. If the phone rang or a car honked its horn, it would not disturb or bother you as you are in both places at the same time.

You are hypnotized whenever you daydream. If someone spoke to you while you were daydreaming, you might not hear a single word. I am sure you have had the experience of driving in your car and then suddenly wondering where the last five miles have gone. This is called *wild hypnosis*. You simply went on automatic pilot while you thought of other things. If something had come up ahead of you, you would have instantly come out of hypnosis and attended to it. You were driving safely after all. People get hypnotized by television and movie screens all the time. I tend to avoid sad movies as I become emotionally involved and start to cry. This means that I've been hypnotized by the film. Consciously, I know that it is simply images on a screen, but I still allow myself to become hypnotized by them.

We drift in and out of hypnosis all the time. If the film is exciting, I'll become engrossed and absorbed in it. If the film goes on and on with very little happening in it, I'll probably come out of hypnosis and become aware of the chair I'm sitting in.

We are all different. I might be engrossed in a particular film, but my wife sitting next to me might be bored and wishing it would end. Consequently, I'm in a state of hypnosis, but she is not.

Hypnotism is not something to fear. It is simply a state that we move in and out of all the time. When you visit a hypnotherapist, he or she is simply guiding you into a hypnotic state so that the right messages can be placed into your subconscious mind. Hypnosis is extremely useful for a wide range of problems such as losing weight, controlling stress, stopping smoking, gaining confidence, and so on.

Many hypnotherapists also conduct past-life regressions. If you decide to go to a hypnotherapist to experience a regression, choose the person carefully. Not every hypnotherapist is interested in the subject. Also, you do not want to waste your time having a session with someone who has no interest in anything other than your money. Find a hypnotherapist who specializes in past-life regressions. This person will be interested in the subject and able to guide you through a regression smoothly and safely.

When people come to me for a past-life regression I always say that they will view disturbing scenes as if they were being played on a television screen and were happening to someone else. Despite this, occasionally someone will experience genuine terror. A hypnotherapist who is used to conducting past-life regressions will know exactly what to do in this type of situation.

It is a good idea to visit a hypnotherapist for your first hypnotic regression. This enables you to experience a past life in a safe environment. Your hypnotherapist is likely to be a sympathetic person who will be prepared to discuss the past life with you afterward. However, it may not be possible for you to do this. There may not be any hypnotherapists in your area, or you may not be able to find one with an interest in past-life regression. You might prefer to do it on your own. Fortunately, it is a simple matter to use hypnotic techniques to experience your past lives on your own.

Hypnotic Regression

There are four stages to a hypnotic regression. The first and most important part of the process is to be able to relax completely. Once you are completely relaxed, the second step is to go back through time to one of your many past lives. The third step is to explore that past lifetime. Finally, you return to the present with all the memories of everything you did in that past life intact.

Step One—Relaxation

Sit or lie down comfortably. Make sure that you are wearing loose-fitting clothes and that the room is reasonably warm. You lose about one degree of body heat during hypnosis. The process will not work if you are shivering. You might like to cover yourself with a blanket.

Some people like to have gentle mood music playing. I prefer the quiet, myself. However, music can help to eliminate any outside distractions. If you have music playing, choose something that has no recognizable tunes as you may find yourself humming along with the music instead of returning to a past life.

It is important to become as relaxed as possible. There are a number of ways of doing this. Taking deep breaths and exhaling slowly is a good method, particularly if you silently tell yourself to relax each time you exhale.

Another method is to tighten and then release each muscle group. You might, for instance, tense your arm muscles as tightly as possible, hold them tensed for several seconds, and then relax them completely.

The method I prefer is to slowly work my way through my body, relaxing every area in turn. I start with my toes and by the time I reach the top of my head I am totally relaxed. I do this by first becoming aware of my toes, and then relaxing them. I then become aware of my feet and relax them as much as possible. I then do the same thing with my ankles, calves, knees, thighs, abdomen, chest, and shoulders, before moving down first one arm and then the other. I then relax the muscles in my neck and face. Finally, I scan my entire body to see if any area is still tense. I focus on relaxing that area, and then spend a few moments enjoying the feeling of complete and total relaxation in every part of my body.

We live in a highly stressful world and often we do not achieve this state of complete and total relaxation even in our sleep. This is why we sometimes wake up in the morning still feeling tired even though we've slept for the usual amount of time. This relaxation exercise is extremely beneficial and is worth practicing, even if you have no desire to use it for exploring your past lives.

Step Two—Back Through Time

There are many ways to move back through time and space to unlock the doors of a past life. The most common method is to imagine yourself walking along a long hallway with doors on both sides. Behind each of these doors is one of your past lives, and you can stop at any one of them, open the door, and move immediately into a past life.

A variation of this method is to imagine yourself coming down a beautiful flight of stairs into a large room. This room is designed purely for you and your own comfort, so you can furnish it in any way you wish. You sit down in a comfortable chair in the middle of the room and look at the different doors that lead off from your room. You know that each one leads to a different past life, and you take your time in deciding which one you want to explore. When you feel ready, you get up, walk across the room, and open the door of your choice.

Another method is to imagine yourself leaving your physical body and floating several hundred feet up into the air. When you are ready, slowly descend and you'll find yourself in another time and place.

A method similar to this is to imagine yourself sitting in the basket of a helium balloon as it takes off. You feel very comfortable and relaxed as it rises higher and higher. You notice that once it is a couple of hundred feet up in the air it gives a slight jolt and then moves back through time and space, finally landing and letting you out into another lifetime.

Instead of heading upward in preparation for a past life, some people prefer to head downward to the past. To do this, all you need to do is imagine a large chute, like a water slide. There is a handle at the top. By turning this handle you change the past life that you will emerge into. When you feel that you have turned the handle in the right direction, sit down on the chute and enjoy sliding back into a past life.

Another method is to imagine yourself on a small boat making its way down the river of life. You can steer the boat to shore whenever you wish. Wherever you choose to stop will be an important occasion in one of your past lives.

A method that many of my clients enjoy is to simply imagine yourself drifting back through time until something causes you to stop. This will be the first faint stirring of a past-life recall, and you can stop moving back whenever you wish to see what is going on.

Some people like to imagine themselves in a beautiful elevator. They push the button for any floor. When the elevator stops they walk out and into one of their past lives.

One man who came to see me wanted to return to a past life in a time capsule. He had a vivid impression of what this looked like in his mind. So once he was fully relaxed, I had him imagine that he was climbing into his time capsule, fastening the seat belts, and closing the door. I then counted from ten down to one, which is when the time capsule took off. He then imagined himself inside the capsule as it hurtled back through time to one of his past lives. Once it landed, he opened the door and stepped out into a past life. When he had satisfied his curiosity with this past life he returned to the present by returning to his time capsule and hurtling back to my office. This method worked so well for him that I have used it a number of times since with different clients. I have also used a time tunnel with some of my clients.

One method that I particularly enjoy is to imagine a beautiful rainbow. It is not an ordinary rainbow as it is possible to walk over it and into a past life. The image of a rainbow is a happy one, so I use this method frequently when a client is nervous about what is going to happen. Rainbows are always fun to see in real life, and the thought of a rainbow helps many people to relax.

In the end, the method that you use to go back to a past life does not matter. All you need to do is imagine yourself going back through time until you are there.

For the sake of completeness, this is what I would say to someone who is returning to a past life by walking down a hallway:

"Just imagine yourself standing at the top of a beautiful staircase. It is the most beautiful staircase you have ever seen. You can feel the soft texture of the luxurious carpet beneath your feet. You feel the freshly polished wood of the handrail, and you decide that you are ready to walk down the staircase to explore one of your many past lives.

"*There are ten steps, and as you hold the handrail and I count from ten down to one, simply allow yourself to double your relaxation with each step you take so that by the time we reach the bottom you'll be totally, completely, absolutely limp, loose, and relaxed.*

"*Ten. Double your relaxation as you move down one step.*

"*Nine. Doubling your relaxation yet again.*

"*Eight. Enjoying this feeling of warmth and peace and total relaxation.*

"*Seven. Drifting down even more now into total relaxation.*

"*Six. Another step down into this wonderful peaceful state.*

"*Five. You are halfway down now, enjoying this wonderful, tranquil relaxation.*

"*Four. More and more relaxed.*

"*Three . . . two . . . and one.*

"*Feeling totally relaxed now as you step off the staircase into a beautiful hallway. It is warm, well-lit, and so peaceful. You walk along the hallway now, gazing curiously at all the doors on both sides of the hallway. Behind each door are the memories of one of your many past lives, and you can stop outside any door you wish.*

"You look at some of the doors more closely, but one door seems to have a greater fascination for you than the others. You pause outside this door, and then raise your hand to turn the handle. You open the door and step into one of your past lifetimes."

Step Three—Explore Your Past Life

The past life you have just returned to will be faint and hard to decipher at first. Simply pause and take a few deep breaths and allow it to come into better focus. Look down at your feet and see what footwear, if any, you are wearing. Then look at your clothing. See if you are male or female. You may not get an answer to this immediately, especially if you are a young child. Sense how your body feels. Does it feel young and full of life? Tired and weary? Warm or cold? This will give you some indication as to your age and state of health. Do you feel happy and contented with life?

Now look around and see if you are indoors or outdoors. Notice if anyone else is with you. See what you are doing.

Now that you are becoming familiar with your new environment, you can move back and forth in time within this past life. Decide what it is you want to experience, count one, two, and three to yourself, and you'll instantly be transported to a new scene. You can explore any aspect of your life by thinking about it and counting up to three.

There are a number of experiences that I always encourage my clients to visualize. I want them to see what they did for a living. I want them to recall at least one incident with the person whom they most loved in that lifetime. I want them to participate in a family scene. I want them to picture a relaxed scene with friends. I also want them to see themselves doing something that made them feel proud. Together these incidents help build up a picture of the person's life. You will find it valuable to ask them too, as you explore your past lives.

Most people want to know what they looked like in a past life. Take yourself to a room that contains mirrors. Of course, you may be experiencing a lifetime in which mirrors did not exist. In this case take yourself to a pond or river and see if you can see your reflection in the water.

The same thing applies if you do not know your name in this lifetime. Take yourself to a scene where someone was calling you and you will immediately know your name.

Take as long as you wish to explore this past life. Before you return to the present, visualize yourself on the last day of the lifetime you are exploring. See what you are doing and who is with you. Find out if you have any regrets. Then see yourself pass over into spirit.

Move back and witness your death in a detached way if it is likely to cause pain or emotion. Look down on the physical body you have just left. This will give you some idea as to how old you were and what your state of health was when you died. You will probably experience a sense of release as you do this. Your spirit will be happy to have finally shed this physical body and be able to move on.

Ask yourself what lessons you had to learn in that particular lifetime. Find out if there is any karma from that past life that is affecting your current life.

Step Four—Return to the Present

Once you have explored your previous life for as long as you wish, it is time to return to the present. Tell yourself that you will recall everything that occurred during your regression, and that new memories will come into your conscious awareness in the next few days. Then bring yourself back to your current life by silently counting from one to five. Keep your eyes closed as you gradually return to the present. When you are ready, count to five again and open your eyes.

People return in different emotional states. Some people are excited, but others are almost depressed. Sit quietly for a few minutes and think about your past life. Give thanks for your ability to uncover your long-lost memories, and also give thanks for the blessings in your current life.

Now that you have uncovered one of your past lives you will be able to return to it as often as you wish. All you need to do at the start of step two is to request that you return to this particular lifetime, and you will immediately go back and be able to explore it further.

Naturally, you will be able to use the same technique to explore other incarnations. At the start of step two tell yourself that you will return to a past life that you have not explored before, and you will go back to a different lifetime.

Helpful Hints

In my office most people go straight back to a past life with little difficulty. This is because they have come to see me with a specific goal in mind, and all I need to do is direct them back to a past life and guide them through it.

However, it is not always as easy as that when you do it on your own. Outside distractions may be a nuisance, particularly if they are created by members of your own family. You may feel guilty about leaving tasks undone. People might come into the room to see what you are doing.

If these problems persist, it is better to abort the past-life regression and attend to them first. You are likely to relax more easily if the washing up has been done, for instance. You might have to choose another time when outside distractions are less likely. You may find that late at night or early in the morning is the best time to experiment.

Some people find that they can relax easily, but then find it hard to return to a past life. If this happens, insert another step between one and two. Once you are relaxed, think about a scene from your earliest childhood. Visualize it as clearly as possible. See what you are doing, who is with you, and where you are. Explore this scene as completely as possible. This additional stage allows you to relax even further before moving back into a past life.

If you still have problems, there is something else you can do. After visualizing the scene from your earliest childhood, allow yourself to think about a period of history that particularly interests you. While you are thinking about what life must have been like at that particular time, you may find yourself spontaneously regressing to a past lifetime. This lifetime may be thousands of years removed from the period of history you were thinking about, but that does not matter. All you have done is insert another step that helped you return to a past lifetime.

There is one final process that you can do if you are still having problems. I have kept this until last as it is incredibly powerful. After visualizing the childhood scene, return to the present and ask for a guide to help you and to remain with you throughout your past life. This guide may be a wise person you know or someone you have read about. It might be an angel or a spirit guide. It makes no difference who it is. You might actually see this person, or you may gain an impression that your guide is present. Ask your guide for help in the journey you are about to undertake. Once you have received your guide's permission, start the experiment from the beginning again. With your guide to help you, you should have no difficulty in returning to a past life. (A method of returning to a past life using your spirit guide as an escort is covered in chapter 15.)

Many people worry about reliving painful incidents during a regression. Life was certainly much more violent and dangerous in the past than it is for most of us nowadays. Consequently, it is always a good idea to tell yourself that you will see everything in a detached manner, almost as if it is happening to someone else. If a particularly traumatic or difficult situation arises, you can always take a step back and observe it impartially. You can also return to the present at any time by counting from one to five.

Some people handle the regression in a detached manner, but then cry afterward. This is an emotional release. Allow this release to take place if it occurs. It can sometimes be painful to release traumas from the past. We all carry a great deal of the past around with us, and it can be emotional when we let it go. Simply cry for as long as necessary. It is an emotional experience to find out who you were and what you were doing in a past life, and it is understandable that these feelings need to be released. Do not try to control or suppress them.

Like all the other methods in this book, practice is required. Some people experience a past-life regression on their first attempt, but other people need to repeat the exercise again and again before they finally succeed.

In a past life you will learn only what the person you used to be knew. So you may not discover the year you were born in, the name of the country you lived in, or the name of the ruling monarch. You may not even know the name of the village you lived in, as you might have called it "home." Sometimes you can gain additional knowledge by looking up details in encyclopedias and history books. Illustrations in these books can be extremely useful as they often depict objects that you saw in your past life but did not pause to identify.

You may identify people in your past life who are important to you in this lifetime. Someone who was your wife in a past life might be your son or mother in this lifetime. The relationships and sexes change, but the person will be instantly recognizable. If this happens, you will notice a subtle change in your relationship with these people in the future. You will become more accepting and understanding of them. You will realize that they are in your present life to help you learn some important lessons. And in the same way, they will be learning from you. You will probably be subconsciously aware of this karmic link anyway, and will find it extremely helpful to have proof of it from your past-life regressions.

Debbie's Experience

Debbie is an eighteen-year-old student who wants to become a doctor. She came to my psychic development classes with her mother. Her mother was bright, vivacious, and rather overpowering. Not surprisingly, Debbie hardly said a word at any of the classes. Yet during the group regression she received faint traces of a past life in Imperial Rome and wanted to explore this lifetime further.

Debbie's mother gave her a past-life regression as a birthday present. Debbie was excited, yet unsure that she really wanted to know more about this past life. We discussed it for a while until she was ready to go ahead.

Debbie was a good hypnotic subject and had no difficulty in returning to a past life. However, it was not in ancient Rome. It was early twentieth-century New York, and she was an elderly woman named Joan who lived in a small apartment with a cat named Rags.

"Has it been a good life?" I asked.

Joan tossed her head and grimaced. "Had its moments," she said. Her voice sounded old and tired. Despite being a nonsmoker, her voice sounded rasping as if she'd smoked a pack of cigarettes every day of her life.

"What was the best time?"

Joan smiled in reminiscence. "When I was eighteen, in Central Park. With Herbie." She coughed and shook her head. "Poor Herbie."

"Who was Herbie?"

"Friend."

"That's all, just a friend?"

Joan giggled, and for a second seemed to be eighteen again. Then her face appeared to age again.

"I loved him."

"Good. And did he love you?"

"Of course." Joan sounded indignant.

"Did you marry him?"

Joan shook her head. "No."

I was about to change the subject, as Joan appeared to be getting upset, when she added, "He's Jewish."

"And that means you can't marry him?"

Joan nodded. Several times she seemed about to say something, but changed her mind. Eventually, I asked her who she married.

"Tommy Pearson."

"Do you love him?"

"He's dead."

"Was it a happy marriage?"

The marriage seemed to be neither good nor bad. They had two children, Walter and Edward. Tommy worked hard as a baker, and eventually owned his own business. He never made much money, but he was a good father and always managed to provide the necessities of life. They were married for almost forty years and only ever had two vacations. One was to Chicago to see the World's Fair, and the other was to a place that sounded like Duesbury. Joan became annoyed with me when I tried to clarify the name. Both vacations were one week long.

Tommy Pearson died two days after his sixtieth birthday. Their older son, Walter, took over the bakery. He was a good worker but a poor businessman, and the business failed a few years later. This caused a major rift in the family and Edward, who worked in a bank, refused to have anything to do with his brother.

"Christmas day I see one boy, and then the other," Joan said. "Never together. One in the morning, one in the afternoon. It's cruel, but families are cruel."

"Did you ever see Herbie again?" I asked.

Joan's eyes sparkled and a smile briefly played on her lips. "Once. In Central Park. Walter and Edward were small, maybe six and four. It was Sunday afternoon, and we were walking, enjoying the sunshine as it had been a long winter. A family outing. I looked across at a park bench and there was Herbie with his arm around a beautiful woman with long dark hair. They looked very happy. Our eyes met and I blushed, and then we walked away. Tommy didn't notice anything. I've often thought of that day and wondered who the beautiful woman was." Joan bit her lip and appeared pensive. "I hope he had a happy life."

Joan was now waiting for death.

"My friends are gone, and my only family are the boys and their children. I see them occasionally. I sit at my window and watch the world go by. Sometimes the days are long, but usually I fall asleep in my chair. Mr. Bernstein next door looks after me. He shops and tells me long stories about his childhood. He's a nice man."

"I'd now like you to go to the last day of the life that you are exploring. You will not have passed over, and you'll see the scene in a detached way, almost as if it's happening to someone else. There'll be no pain and no emotion. Are you there?"

"I'm in my chair at the window. I've got a pain."

"Where?"

Joan indicated her heart. "Something's wrong."

"What are you doing?"

"Nothing."

"Why don't you ask Mr. Bernstein to help?"

Joan shook her head impatiently. "He's dead."

"Who else can help?"

"I don't want help. I'm ready."

"Okay. Again, seeing the scene in a detached manner, I want you to see yourself a few moments after you experienced physical death. Can you see the body you've just left?"

Joan smiled. "It's so small!"

"Is there anyone else there?"

Joan shook her head.

"Looking back on that lifetime, is there any karma that is affecting your current life?"

Most people have to think about this question before answering it, but Debbie's reply was instant. "Follow your dreams. Don't let other people influence you. Don't settle for second best."

I returned her to the present, and after a few seconds, woke her up. Debbie was surprised with her past life.

"It's not what I expected at all," she said. "I thought I'd be rich and married to the man of my dreams. I seemed to miss out both ways."

"So you'll marry for love this time?"

Debbie laughed. "This time I'll marry Herbie."

"Did you recognize him?"

Debbie shook her head. "No. I haven't met him yet. But we're meant to be together. I'll know him when we find each other."

"He is your soul mate?"

"You know, in that regression I felt that I had known Herbie for many, many lifetimes. We seemed to be so close, and yet we were not allowed to be together. It seemed so cruel." She shook her head. "That won't happen this time."

7

Scrying Your
Past Lives

*Being born twice is no more remarkable than being
born once.*

Voltaire (1694–1778)

Scrying is a little-practiced art in the West
nowadays. The word *scry* comes from the
medieval word *descry*, which means "to make
out something dimly," or "to discern something that is not clear." One hundred years ago
crystal-ball gazing was popular, and many

people still expect to find a lady sitting behind a large crystal ball when they go for a psychic reading. Cartoonists commonly portray psychic readers as garishly dressed Gypsies gazing intently into their crystal balls and expressing profound words such as, "No future, but what a past!"

Scrying is believed to have originated in Persia. In Egypt scrying was done by gazing into a pool of ink or even blood. The ancient Greeks scryed by gazing into pools of water or a polished metal mirror. Saint Augustine, Pliny, and Saint Thomas Aquinas all mentioned this art in their writings. Early in the sixteenth century, Paracelsus wrote *How to Conjure the Crystal So That All Things May Be Seen in It.*

Nostradamus (1503–1566) is probably the most famous scryer of all time. Most of his famous quatrains were composed after gazing into a brass bowl filled with water. Nostradamus also used a hand mirror when he needed greater detail. The celebrated John Dee, astrologer to Queen Elizabeth I, is also known to have used crystal balls and mirrors. Intriguingly, he never gazed into the crystal ball himself. An assistant did the scrying while John Dee wrote down the visions.

Fortunately, you do not need a crystal ball to scry your own past lives. In Tibet, smooth black stones are used. In India, I've seen people gazing into a small bowl of India ink. I've also seen Indian women scrying with their thumb nails. In the past, white, yellow, green, blue, violet, and transparent crystals were commonly used. Mirrors work just as well also. In fact, many people prefer to scry with a mirror than with a ball. All you really need is something to focus on.

Scrying with a Glass of Water

A glass of water works just as well as a crystal ball. I collect antique crystal balls. One Victorian specimen in my collection is a circular hollow ball that was filled with water. It rests on a stand that conceals where the water was inserted. Gradually over the last hundred years, some of the water has escaped and now the ball is only three-quarters full. Anyone who used that particular crystal ball was actually scrying with a glass of water without knowing it.

Step One—Preparation

Use a plain, simple, round tumbler filled almost to the top with water. Place this glass in a position where you can sit and gaze at it without raising or lowering your head. Your eyes should be about three feet away from it.

Step Two—Gaze into the Glass

Take several deep breaths and gaze at the glass. After a few minutes the water will appear to become milky, almost like a fine mist. Keep on gazing steadily at it, and in time this mist will become a faint blue. There is no need to concentrate on the glass of water. Simply stare at it, thinking in general terms about your desire to return to a past life. Your mind will wander at times. This is perfectly normal, and there is no need to worry about it. Once you become aware of this, direct your thoughts back to your goal and wait for the mist to appear.

Step Three—Return to a Past Life

Think of your purpose in returning to one of your past lives. Shortly you will see vague shapes appearing in the bluish mist. If you are extremely fortunate, you may be able to witness one of your past lives unfolding on the screen of mist, almost as if you are watching it on a television screen. However, this is unlikely unless you are extremely good at visualization.

Most people find that memories of their past lives appear in their minds as they gaze at the swirling mist. It is important to remain as calm and relaxed as you can. Virtually everyone I know who has practiced this method has had the experience of becoming excited when the past-life memories began. As soon as they start thinking consciously about what is going on, the thoughts disappear. So remain tranquil and relaxed and gaze into the glass in an almost detached, indifferent manner. You can always get excited afterward, once you have caught hold of your long-lost memories.

Step Four—Return to the Present

The glass of water seems to know when you have seen enough. The scene will gradually cloud over to tell you that the session has come to an end. Silently give thanks for the opportunity to return to a past life, take several deep breaths, and then get up.

It is possible for several people to gaze into the glass at the same time. Interestingly, each of them will return to a valid past life. I was slightly skeptical about this to begin with. I had experimented with thought transmission between two people using the same crystal ball, and felt that somehow everyone would pick up the same images. However, this is not the case, and if you wish, you and your friends can scry together at the same time.

Scrying with a Mirror

You can use a mirror in the same way as a glass of water or a crystal ball. Naturally, the mirror should be of good quality and be kept as clean as possible. The same thing applies if you are using a crystal ball: it should be kept clean and covered in black or blue velvet when not in use.

Step One—Preparation

It is best to seat yourself slightly lower than the mirror so that you are not staring at yourself. From where you are sitting, the mirror should not reflect anything other than a blank wall. The room should be in semi-darkness. I find it helpful to pull the drapes and use a pair of candles, one on each side of the mirror, for illumination.

Step Two—Gaze into the Mirror

Gaze into the mirror in exactly the same way that you stared at the glass of water. In time you will notice a fine cloud of white fog form. This is usually denser than the mist that surrounds a crystal ball or glass of water.

Step Three—Return to a Past Life

Keep on gazing at the mirror and allow the memories of your past life to return. You may witness scenes unfolding inside the mirror, or you may sense them in your mind. Most people sense the scenes rather than see them, but some people are able to do both. They start by sensing the scenes and then, with practice, gradually develop the ability to see them in the mirror. This is the reason why I prefer a mirror to a glass of water or a crystal ball; it allows the pictures to be shown on a much larger area.

Step Four—Return to the Present

After a while, the scene will cloud over and you will not be able to see any more. This may happen after a minute or two, while on other occasions you will be able to see visions for an hour or more.

Once the scene clouds over, realize that the experience is over for the moment. It is a waste of time trying to return to it at this session. Take several deep breaths and thank the mirror before returning to your everyday life.

How to Make a Scrying Mirror

A true scrying mirror is black. It is easy to make one of these. All you need is the glass that covers the face of a clock. You can buy these from a clock repairer or even from a craft store. Choose one that is about five inches in diameter. Clean the glass thoroughly, and then paint the outside of it (convex side) with black paint. When it is dry you will be able to use the inside of the glass as a black mirror. Keep your mirror wrapped in a black cloth when it is not in use.

Choosing a Crystal Ball

Crystal balls are extremely expensive. Glass balls work just as well, and can be purchased from New Age bookstores and occult suppliers. Even cheaper are acrylic balls which are available at the same stores.

However, acrylic balls need to be treated with great care as they mark easily. I find that they work perfectly until the surface gets marked or scratched. If you look after them carefully, they will serve you well.

It is best to start out with a simple glass of water or a mirror, black or plain, before investing large sums of money in scrying equipment. Look after whatever you use. Practice regularly, and see what comes into your conscious awareness. Take notes of your progress and of the results. You will find that the more you practice, the better you become. In time you will be able to scry for many other purposes, such as finding lost objects and seeing into the future, in addition to reliving your past lives.

There are a number of things you can do if you are having difficulty. Wait until you see the milky mist surrounding the ball. Turn away and count to ten slowly. You should still be able to see the mist when you turn back. If the mist appears to have disappeared, wait until it returns and try again.

If you can see the mist but nothing appears on it, turn away and look at a brightly colored object in the room for fifteen seconds. Turn back and see if you can superimpose the image of the object you were looking at onto the mist. Once you are successful at this, recall an incident that happened in your past and see if you can place that onto the screen of mist. Once you are able to do this successfully you should have no further difficulty in visualizing your past lives in the ball.

Melvin's Experience

Melvin is a twenty-three-year-old bank clerk who attended my psychic development classes several years ago with his girlfriend, Alice. She was outgoing, but he was shy and reserved. His father had been a clock repairer and Melvin had a large supply of clock glasses at home. He made black mirrors for everyone in the class. He did not, however, experiment with one until after his girlfriend had experienced positive results.

"It was easier than I thought," he told us. "I had the glass in my pocket and I was in the lunchroom at work all by myself. Alice kept telling me about her past lives, so I thought I'd give it a try. I moved close to the window and gazed into the mirror. The mist began so quickly that I changed positions, thinking it was something to do with the light.

"Then I saw a draped figure in the mirror. It was a man on horseback, and I watched him galloping down a wooded glade. At the end was a huge house. The man rode past the house to some stables, and someone helped him dismount. Then a small child ran towards him, calling out 'Dadda!' He turned and a huge grin spread over his face. He kneeled down and the little girl came running into his arms."

Melvin paused and looked around the class. His eyes were gleaming. "The man on the horse was me and my daughter was Alice."

Alice had explored many of her previous lives, and one of them appeared to be the same one that Melvin had unlocked. "I was a little girl, wearing an ornate, brocaded dress. I was in a library. All the books were for grownups, but I was happy because this was Dadda's room. I could sense his presence, even though he wasn't there. I sat at his desk, and then I stood at the window looking out into the rain. I knew he would be home soon. I fell asleep, with my forehead against the glass. I woke up when Mamma came in and picked me up.

"'Where's Dadda?' I asked.

"'Shh, little girl,' my mother said. 'He'll be home soon.'

"I went back to sleep and Mamma put me to bed. Later I woke when Dadda came into the room to kiss me goodnight. He sat on the bed and told me a fairy story till I fell asleep."

"And the Dadda was me!" Melvin said.

It is not unusual for two people who are close to each other in this lifetime to find themselves in different relationships to each other in previous lives. The people are always recognizable, even though sexes and relationships change.

Melvin was obviously a natural with the scrying mirror. All the same, he went about it in the right way. He was relaxed and had no great expectations. He simply allowed the past life to come through. If he had been anxious, or had approached the task with grim determination, the experiment might have been a failure.

Melvin and Alice are still together. This is not surprising, as there is obviously a strong karmic link between them. I believe they are soul mates. They have uncovered several other lifetimes in which they both featured, as well as other lifetimes in which they did not find each other.

Melvin and Alice both use a scrying mirror to recover their past-life memories. Melvin found he could return to his past lifetimes just as easily using other methods, but prefers the scrying mirror as it is quick and convenient. Alice enjoys mirror scrying more than the other methods, but I feel that this is probably because Melvin made her scrying mirror for her.

8

Tick-Tock Regression

And since I have lost much time with this age,
I would be glad, as God shall give me leave,
To recover it with posterity.

Sir Francis Bacon (1561–1626)

Not surprisingly, clocks and images of clocks have been used frequently to help people return to their past lives. The steady ticking of a clock is a reminder that time is passing by. Unless we become aware of it for some reason, the ticking of a clock is usually not heard. When it is noticed, people are often surprised at how loud it actually is.

I became aware of how useful a clock was in regression work by accident. I replaced the clock in my office with one that gave a much louder ticking sound than its predecessor. It occurred to me that the sound it made was soothing and restful, and experimented to see if people preferred it to the gentle music I had previously used when putting people into hypnosis. As most people liked it, I gave up using the taped music and now use the ticking of the clock as a background to my voice when putting people into hypnosis.

I also experimented with these methods of returning to a past life in my workshops and classes. A few people found them to be the quickest and easiest way of recovering their long-lost memories. However, most people found them more difficult than the other methods. I am including them here for the sake of completeness. They are worth experimenting with as they are highly effective methods for some people.

There are two distinct ways of returning to a past life using the sound of a clock.

Ticking Clock: Method One
Step One—Relax to the Sound of a Ticking Clock
The first step is to relax somewhere with your eyes closed and with a ticking clock nearby. Ideally, you do

not want any other distracting sounds to interfere with your concentration.

Step Two—Think of Previous Incidents

Think back over your life and recall any incidents that you can remember that involved a clock. It does not matter what types of incidents they are. It might be watching the clock at work slowly ticking away the last few minutes of the working day. You might picture a scene in which you are lying in bed waiting for the alarm to go off.

I remember panicking in a library many years ago when the clock indicated closing time before I had selected any books to read. As a teenager I spent many happy hours at the local swimming baths and could never believe how quickly the large clock at the end of the pool raced through the hours. My father had a collection of clocks, and I have strong memories of waking up during the night and hearing different clocks striking the hour, one after the other. I always found these sounds soothing, and quickly drifted back to sleep. Whenever I do this exercise, these are the scenes I recall.

Step Three—Take Several Deep Breaths and Return to a Past Life

Once you have remembered several incidents involving clocks, take several deep breaths and allow yourself to drift back through time and space to an experience you had in a past lifetime involving the sound of a clock. Once you are there you can proceed to explore the past life for as long as you wish.

Step Four—Return to the Present

When you are ready you can return to the present in one of two different ways. You can think about the incidents you remembered in this lifetime before you returned to a past life, gradually bringing yourself back to the present. Alternatively, you can take several deep breaths, count silently from one to five, and then open your eyes.

Ticking Clock: Method Two

Step One—Stare at the Clock's Face

Sit down directly in front of a ticking clock. The clock should be directly in front of you so that you can look at its face without raising, lowering, or turning your head. Gaze steadily at the clock for five minutes.

Step Two—Close Your Eyes and Picture the Clock

Close your eyes and see if you can clearly see the clock in your mind. If you can visualize the clock in complete detail, you can proceed to the next step. If you fail to see the clock vividly in your mind, open your eyes again and stare at the clock for another five minutes. Repeat until you are able to visualize the clock clearly in your mind.

Step Three—Remove the Hands

Once you can see the clock clearly in your mind, mentally remove the minute hand from the clock while continuing to see the remainder of the clock. Next, mentally remove the hour hand so that you are looking at the face and casing, free of any hands.

Step Four—Remove the Numbers

Mentally remove the numbers one by one. I prefer to start at number twelve and move backward until finally number one is removed. You may prefer to remove them in a clockwise direction, or perhaps take them off in a random order. It makes no difference, as long as all the numbers are removed one at a time. Finally, mentally remove any other markings on the clock face, such as the maker's name. Once the face is empty, allow it to slowly fade away until it has vanished. Finally, watch the casing fade away until the entire clock has disappeared from your mind.

Step Five—Drift Back to a Past Lifetime

After the clock has disappeared, take several deep breaths and allow yourself to drift back into another lifetime. The purpose of this exercise is to allow you to reach the right state of peace and tranquility so that returning to a past life becomes a simple thing to do.

Step Six—Return to the Present

When you are ready to return to your everyday life, take five deep breaths. Allow yourself to gradually become familiar with your surroundings, and then open your eyes.

It is unlikely that you will be successful at either of these exercises on the first attempt. However, with regular practice, you will find it becoming easier and easier to relax to the extent necessary for success. And one day you will do the exercise and suddenly find yourself back in a past life. Once you have succeeded once, you will be able to do it again whenever you wish.

Carl's Experience

Carl is a well-to-do businessman in his late fifties. He has married and divorced twice, and came to my classes hoping to learn something about his purpose in life. He always stood out in my classes as he was usually the only person wearing a business suit. Although he was a naturally friendly person, it took him a long while to relax and mix freely with the other people in the class. He told me later that he had spent a lifetime in business meetings where he had learned to express very little of what he was really thinking. Consequently, he found a class full of people talking openly about their experiences and feelings hard to fit into.

Carl became fascinated with the idea that he had lived before. The concept of reincarnation had never occurred to him before coming to my classes. He read everything he could find on the subject, and tried several methods of returning to a past life on his own.

On the evening we did a group regression, Carl was excited and nervous. I recall that about three-quarters of the class went back to a previous lifetime, but Carl was not one of them. He was incredibly disappointed and considered himself a failure.

After the class he stayed behind to ask me some questions. I pointed out that he had probably tried too hard. If he had simply relaxed and allowed it to happen, he might well have succeeded. He agreed that this was most likely the problem, and then told me about the other methods he had tried.

"What other method can I practice at home?" he asked.

I told him that in a few weeks we would be doing the tick-tock method in class, and that he could practice with it on his own if he desired. He was pleased to learn of yet another method of regression, and left feeling slightly more optimistic.

When he returned the following week he was radiant.

"I've done it!" he exclaimed to everyone as they arrived for the class. "I know two of my past lives!"

He was so excited about it that I asked him to tell everyone about his experience.

After the previous lesson, he had gone home and read for an hour before going to bed. He did not feel in the least bit tired, so he lay in bed and visualized a clock on the ceiling above his head. He found this easy to do. He gradually made different parts of the clock disappear until it totally vanished.

"I took ten deep breaths," he told us. "I was scared that I'd get no further as the first part was so easy. Suddenly, I was a small child sitting in front of the fire in my grandmother's living room. She wasn't in the room with me, but I knew she was my granny. Behind me I could hear her grandfather clock ticking.

"I knew that I was who I am now, but at the same time I was also that little boy two hundred years ago. I was somewhere in Europe, probably the Netherlands judging by the furniture.

"I could hear Granny in the kitchen singing a song as she prepared dinner. It was a sad song, but I thought it was beautiful. I went through to the kitchen and hugged her skirts. She laughed and hugged me back.

"'So my little man's coming back to life again,' she said. Then I remembered everything. I was out one day with my mother and father, and father got into an argument with someone. A fight began and he was stabbed. He fell to the ground, and the other man ran off. My mother hugged my father as his blood formed an ever-larger pool on the cobblestones. I stood back, staring, unable to do anything.

"Finally—it must have been quickly, but it seemed like forever—other people ran to help, but it was too late. My mother stood up and wailed. It was high-pitched and sounded like a wild animal. She looked at me, but her eyes showed no recognition. I took a step towards her, but the look on her face made me pause. Then I turned and ran.

"People found me by the river two days later. My grandmother took me in. I learned later that my mother was in an asylum. She died there a few years later.

"Granny became my mother, and she doted on me. I became a lawyer, thanks to her urging and encouragement. She lived a long life, and I looked after her in her old age."

Carl looked around the room, smiling broadly. "I can see it all as clearly as I can see any of you," he said.

"It's the most remarkable thing that's ever happened to me, in this lifetime, anyway."

"Was it a happy life?" I asked. "Did you have a wife and children?"

Carl shook his head. "No. There never seemed to be any special person for me. I spent most of my time working, but I was happy. I was really happy."

"You mentioned two past lives," one of the other students said.

Carl nodded. "You're right. I did it again the next morning, when I woke up, and went back to the same past life. I thought I'd do it again that evening, but instead of returning to that lifetime I went back to a much earlier life.

"I haven't got a musical bone in my body, but in that life I seemed to be a troubadour or a minstrel, something like that. It must have been England. I travelled around, singing songs and making people laugh, and they gave me money. Sometimes I was on my own. At other times I was part of a group. I didn't seem to have a home. In the winter I went south and west and waited for the weather to come right again so I could start on my travels once more.

"I think it was a reasonably happy life. It wasn't a long one. I got a chill and died under a hedge, miles from anywhere. It was raining, almost like a blizzard, and I was happy to leave that life behind."

Carl turned to me. "There was no wife or partner in that life either," he said. "Is this why I've been divorced twice in this one?"

I shook my head. "It won't be as neat as that. You must have had many other lifetimes as well. You'll have to examine many more to see if the absence of a partner is a common factor in most of them."

For no apparent reason I had assumed that Carl was happy living on his own. In fact, he was desperately looking for a partner. That was no doubt one of the reasons why he came to my classes as most of the students were women.

Over the following weeks Carl returned to many previous lifetimes. Interestingly, no matter whether he was male or female, he seemed to always be without a partner.

Eventually, Carl found a lifetime with a partner. He seemed to be in central Asia, living at a subsistence level. His wife seemed to be always ill. Despite this, she produced one child every year. Almost all of them died before they were three years old.

Carl treated her with contempt and had strong memories of endlessly screaming abuse at her. He raped her constantly and beat her up whenever he got drunk. This was not often as drink was a luxury they could seldom afford. One night, however, he went too far and almost killed her in a drunken rage.

Then when he was asleep, she picked up a club and killed him.

Carl found it hard to relate this lifetime to the class. "How could I have been like that?" he asked. "In all my other lives I was a caring, gentle person. Yet in that life, I was a brute."

It is hard to answer questions like that. Perhaps Carl has come back again and again to atone for his evilness in that lifetime. Perhaps he has not enjoyed a stable relationship since then because of the way he treated his wife.

After the lesson Carl told me that he had not been a good husband in either of his marriages. "Work got in the way much of the time," he said. "I'm definitely a workaholic. Also, I had affairs during both marriages. I guess I'm a very slow learner."

Carl is still trying to find a partner. However, he now has a much clearer picture of where he has been in the past, and where he wants to go in the future.

Carl was the only person in that particular class who had success with the tick-tock technique. In fact, he used it constantly as he was not prepared to risk failure again by trying another method. I think he knew consciously that this would not have happened. However, he was not prepared to put it to the test.

9

Fascinations, Skills, and Interests

Births have brought us richness and variety,
And other births will bring us richness and variety . . .

Walt Whitman

We all have innate skills and talents. Some people are born with practical skills. Naturally, they are most successful in practical types of occupations. Other people are born with a natural rhythm or feeling for music. They might become singers, dancers, or musicians. One lady

I know was born with a natural ability to comfort and nurture others. She became a nurse and now runs a geriatric hospital.

Where do these built-in skills come from? Heredity can claim some part in this, but frequently a child is born with a skill or talent that does not seem to come from anywhere. I believe that these skills were honed in previous lifetimes. This helps to explain the phenomenon of child geniuses.

Mozart may well have been a musician in many previous lifetimes before he was born again as Wolfgang Amadeus Mozart. At the age of four he could play the piano competently and was composing pieces for it just one year later. Mozart was born into a musical family, and his father was a composer, violinist, and musical author.

However, George Frideric Handel's family was the complete opposite. None of his ancestors appeared to have been musical. His father was a barber-surgeon who opposed his son's interest in music and wanted him to become a lawyer. His mother gave him no support either, yet he grew up to become the composer of such immortal works as the *Water Music Suite* and the *Messiah.* His remarkable talent had nothing to do with heredity.

Socrates and Plato believed that all knowledge was actually recollection. Henry Ford agreed with this when he said, "Genius is experience. Some seem to think that it is a gift or talent, but it is the fruit of long experience in many lives. Some are older souls than others, and so they know more."[1]

One interesting example that adds credence to this hypothesis concerns Sir William Hamilton (1730–1803). He became an eminent diplomat and antiquarian. While still a child, he wrote a letter to the Persian ambassador. However, he did not write it in modern Persian. His letter was written in an ancient script that had not been used for centuries.[2] This was just one of thirteen languages that he could speak by the time he was thirteen. Where did he gain all of this knowledge from?

Xenoglossy is the ability to speak a foreign language that has not been consciously learned. It is an extremely rare phenomenon, but a number of cases have been investigated. One of these concerns Viviane Silvino, who was born in São Paulo in 1963. Although Portuguese is the language spoken in Brazil, Viviane began speaking phrases in Italian. Before she turned two, she called her sister *mia sorella* and her doll *bambola*. On one occasion her mother told someone that she knew no one who spoke Italian. Viviane promptly said, *"Lo parlo,"* which means "I speak it." As she grew older, the reason for Viviane's knowledge of Italian became apparent. Over a period of time, Viviane began to recall experiences from a past life in Rome during World

War II. Viviane had a fear of airplanes and this was a result of the air raids she had experienced in her previous life.[3]

The famous actor Glenn Ford was able to speak fluent French when hypnotically regressed back to a past life in the court of King Louis XIV. In everyday life he could speak only a few sentences in French, but when regressed he spoke the Parisian French of the 1670s.[4]

If all knowledge is actually recollection, you have at your disposal a number of interests and talents that can provide you with insights into your past lives. I have already mentioned a regular client of mine who has always been good with his hands in every lifetime we have explored. The talent he was born with was manual dexterity, and this has developed over many incarnations so that now his hands can do almost anything.

What skills do you have? Are you the person in the family that everyone comes to when things are going wrong? Do you have a talent for math, or an interest in a certain period of history? Do you collect things? Perhaps a hobby or interest will provide clues about your past lives.

A friend of mine who is a retired army officer has memories of many famous battles in the past, including the Battle of Hastings. Obviously, in this lifetime a military career was the most sensible choice for him to have made as he was continuing a career that may have begun thousands of years ago. There have been a number of famous people in the military who have recalled previous lives, including General George Patton and Air Chief Marshal Lord Dowding, who wrote an excellent book on reincarnation called *Lychgate*. Napoleon Bonaparte believed that he had lived many times before, including lifetimes as Emperor Charlemagne and Alexander the Great.

A young relative of mine has always been fascinated with anything to do with ancient Greece. He knew all the Greek myths and legends at an early age, and continues to learn anything he can about this ancient civilization. Not surprisingly, when I regressed him back to a past life he went directly back to a lifetime in Crete some 2,500 years ago.

You may have to think carefully to determine the special talents that you have. Most people tend to underrate themselves and feel that they have no special strengths or talents. Ask people who know you well to point out your special attributes. You may be surprised at what they tell you.

It is interesting how often skills that are used later on in life become apparent at a very early age. I always wanted to be a writer, and had a small local newspaper that I distributed to my neighbors every week. One of my childhood friends liked to play "shops." When she grew up she went into the retail industry and now owns a successful chain of clothing stores. Is it possible that she learned the essential skills of retailing in her past lives? Think carefully about your own childhood interests, as they may provide you with positive leads about your past lives. Even childhood games can provide clues to past lives.

Take some time to think about your interests. Perhaps write them down if you feel it will help. What types of food do you like? Of course, a love for pizza and pasta does not necessarily indicate a past life in Italy, but it could be a clue. However, if you find that several of your likes and interests also relate to Italy, you quite possibly did spend at least one lifetime in Italy. This is the advantage of writing everything down. Otherwise you might not notice how a certain geographical region or time period keeps cropping up.

Is there something that you always wanted to do, but have never had the opportunity to pursue it? If, for example, you always wanted to play the piano, you may be trying to continue with something that was begun in a previous life. This is particularly likely if you have a strong attraction to piano music composed at a certain time.

Aversions and blocks can also provide valuable clues. If you were punished for doing something in a previous lifetime, you may have a strong desire to keep away from whatever it was in this incarnation. One of my clients was tortured and almost killed in a previous lifetime for insisting that dowsing rods were not the work of the devil. In this lifetime he refused to handle dowsing rods until after the block had been discovered and removed. He is now an extremely good dowser, and so he should be because he has at least two lifetimes of dowsing experience behind him.

Talent Meditation

Step One—Think About Your Talents

Once you know what your talents, skills, and interests are, all you need to do is meditate on them. Sit down somewhere where you will not be disturbed, close your eyes, and think about your specific talents. Think about the pleasure you receive when you practice these skills. Think about what you would like to do with these special gifts in the future. Think about times in the past when you were recognized or appreciated for your talent. This recognition may not have come from others. It may have come from inside you, such as an occasion when you knew you had done something really well. You may be surprised at what comes back to you.

When I think about music in this way, my mind takes me back to an occasion where I played the piano and conducted the choir at a Sunday school concert when I was seventeen. I had completely forgotten about this afternoon until I did this exercise, and it came back as clearly as if it was yesterday. During the concert I was aware that I was doing a good job, and the congratulations of others reinforced those positive feelings. But over time the incident had been forgotten. By doing this exercise, you will probably also recover forgotten memories.

Step Two—Think About Earlier Memories Involving Your Talent or Skill

Take your time and relive these memories for as long as you wish. Each time you finish thinking about a pleasant memory from the past, see if you can go back to a previous incident that utilized these skills.

You will find that each time you do this experiment, more information will come back to you. One day while doing this exercise I remembered an incident involving music that occurred when I was in the first grade. Miss Donald, my teacher, had a variety of musical instruments in a cupboard in the corner of the classroom. I was fascinated with them. One day I gathered up enough confidence to ask her when we would be playing them. She replied that this would happen when all the students learned to be quiet enough in class. Sadly, this never happened and we never got to play the instruments. Again, this is an incident that I had forgotten, even though it had been extremely important at the time. I was desperate to play the instruments, but had not been allowed to.

Step Three—Allow the Talent to Take You Back to a Past Life

Once you have located the earliest possible memory relating to your talent or skill, see if you can go back even further. There is no need to worry if nothing comes into your mind when you do this. You may have to repeat this exercise many times before an earlier memory comes back to you. This might be a memory from a past incarnation, but it may also be a memory from your present life. If so, think about it, enjoy reliving it, and then see if you can go back still further. By doing this, I remembered my mother singing me to sleep when I was little more than a baby. You will be amazed at what memories will come into your mind when you allow enough time for this exercise.

Finally, there will be no more memories relating to your talent from this lifetime. However, there will be many memories from previous lifetimes that are simply waiting to be discovered. Remain calm, but quietly confident that these memories will come back to you. The first time I did this I saw nothing but heard the music of Haydn and was convinced that I was playing a violin in the orchestra. I have never played the violin in this lifetime, but was certain that that was what I was doing. Repeated sessions gradually clarified the scene, and I found myself in a beautiful room, again playing the music of Haydn to a small audience of about twenty people. I was happy, enjoying the music and being part of a small chamber orchestra. The members of the orchestra were all my friends, and we enjoyed playing together. The conductor was a young man I did not know, but he obviously had a great empathy for the music and we all enjoyed working with him.

I know people who have done this exercise once and effortlessly returned to a previous life, but most people find it takes much longer than that. Based on my experience you are more likely to receive faint traces of a past life that gradually become clearer each time you repeat this exercise. Of course, once you have successfully uncovered one memory, you can then move on and explore the life in as much detail as you wish.

Step Four—Return to the Present

Explore the past lifetime for as long as you wish. When you feel it is time to return to the present, take several deep breaths and become aware of where you are sitting or lying. Reassure yourself that now that you have uncovered this past life you will be able to return to it again as often as you wish. When you feel ready, open your eyes.

Judelle's Experience

Judelle is a grade-school teacher. In her spare time she is a potter. Her pottery has won several awards and she sells much of what she produces. She wanted to find out if her natural talent with clay was a product of many past lives or was something new this time around.

She sat in the sun outside her studio, closed her eyes, and went back in time. She thought of the time when she first won an award, and how proud she was. She then went back to an occasion when her teacher at school complimented her on her work. The next memory was when she was seven years old. The family was away on vacation and Judelle made friends with a woman who was a well-known local potter. She allowed Judelle to form clay on her wheel, and, seeing the burgeoning interest in the young child, fired one of Judelle's first pieces for her to take home.

Judelle then tried to go back further. Nothing came into her mind. She waited patiently for several minutes. She was about to give up when she felt a rocking sensation and realized that she was sitting in a boat on the Nile River. She looked down on the rowers working in unison and realized that she was someone important. It seemed too much effort to think about it, so she lay back on the luxurious cushions and gazed imperiously at the people working on the river bank. Her mind fastened on the fact that some of them were loading clay, but the thought immediately passed by.

The boat ride seemed to go on forever, but eventually they moored at a small jetty. A party of people were waiting for her. She could tell they were nervous. They escorted her to a temple that was half finished. Near the entrance she paused and watched a young woman forming a cup out of clay. She knew the party was anxious to go inside, but she was entranced by the way the goblet was formed out of a lump of clay. She picked up some clay and began to mold it. She was aware of the consternation she was causing, and this spurred her on.

Time stood still for her as she kneaded and molded the clay. She did not stop until her father appeared on the steps of the temple. He was not amused at his daughter's behavior and angrily signaled the party to come inside. Reluctantly, Judelle put aside her piece of clay and listlessly walked up the steps and into the temple.

"That didn't all come in one session," Judelle told me. "I got small traces of it first, and then it gradually appeared, not always when I was consciously thinking about it either." She shook her head. "It's the strangest thing, but those memories are so clear and vivid. You wouldn't think they were thousands of years old!"

Since then, Judelle has uncovered a number of past lives in which her feel and love for pottery has been evident. Knowing this has increased her motivation to become a full-time potter and to make as much progress as she can with it in this lifetime.

10

Dowsing Your Past Lives

I am confident that there truly is such a thing as living again, that the living spring from the dead, and that the souls of the dead are in existence.

Socrates (469–399 B.C.E.)

Dowsing is the ability to find something that is hidden, usually something such as water or a mineral that is underground. However, this ability can be used to locate anything at all. For instance, I regularly use it to find items that have been lost by my children. Dowsers traditionally use a forked stick, but a variety of objects can be used. Some people are able to dowse with their hands. Uri Geller is an excellent example of someone who dowses this way.[1]

Dowsing is very old. Deep in the Tassili-n-Ajjer caves in southeast Libya are pictographs showing a group of people watching a dowser using a forked stick. These drawings are estimated to be eight thousand years old.[2]

Anyone can learn to dowse. However, some people are naturally better at it than others. Children take to it naturally, but adults sometimes need to learn to suspend disbelief in order to dowse successfully. In extreme cases I have found that if a successful dowser rests his or her hand on one of the student's shoulders, the dowsing response will happen. Although you don't hear as much about dowsing nowadays as you used to, there are dowsers everywhere. Chapters of the American Society of Dowsers can be found in virtually every state, and if you contact them you will meet many enthusiastic dowsers. They are friendly people who will be happy to help you.

Obviously, if we can dowse for anything that is hidden, we can just as easily dowse for our past lives. Dowsing can be used on its own, or in conjunction with other methods. In fact, I often use dowsing in conjunction with a hypnotic regression to provide a clearer picture of certain past lives.

Dowsers use a variety of implements. The easiest instruments to use when dowsing for past lives are angle rods and the pendulum.

Angle Rods

There are two main ways to dowse for past lives. The first method is to use angle rods. Angle rods are two L-shaped pieces of metal wire. Mine are twelve by six inches. You can buy commercially made angle rods at many New Age stores, but it is easy to make your own from metal coathangers. Hold them loosely in your hands at chest height, with the twelve-inch sections facing forward and parallel to each other. You can ask the angle rods questions that can be answered by either "yes" or "no." When I do this my angle rods cross over each other to indicate a "yes" response, and usually do not move at all to answer "no."

You will need to test your rods to determine what response they will give to you. To do this, you need to ask a series of questions and see what response your angle rods give. Here are the questions to ask:

"Is my name _____?"
"Am I _____ years old?"
"Do I live at [*address*]?"

The first time you ask these questions you need to provide correct information about your name, age, and address. The angle rods should give the same "yes" response each time.

Ask the same questions again, but this time give false information. The angle rods should give you the same negative response to all three questions.

Finally, ask the questions in a random order, giving correct information some of the time, and false information at others. By the time you have done this, you should know how your angle rods respond to indicate positive and negative answers.

Holding the angle rods in your closed fists takes time and practice. The rods must be held loosely, so that they will move to indicate a response. Many people hold them too tightly, and consequently do not receive any response. The remedy for this is to disassemble a couple of cheap ballpoint pens and place the short sides of your angle rods into the barrels. You can grip these as tightly as you wish, but the angle rods will still be able to move loosely inside the plastic casing.

Once you have become used to using your angle rods you can start asking them questions about your previous lifetimes.

Step One—Determining When You Lived Before

Start by asking if you were born in the twentieth century in your most recent life. If the answer is negative, ask the same question about the nineteenth century. Keep on going back through time until you receive a positive response.

Then ask if you were born in the first half of that century. If not, ask about the second half of the century. You already know that this answer will be positive, but it doesn't hurt to check.

Ask about the different decades, and finally ask if you were born in specific years until you receive a positive response. If you wish, you can then determine your month and day of birth in the same way. Most of the time I do not bother to do this at this stage and only do it later if it is likely to help me verify details of this past life.

Of course, you may not necessarily wish to explore your most recent past life. You might want to explore a lifetime that created karma that is affecting your current life. You might want to explore the most recent life you spent with your current partner. All you need to do is ask for what you want and then go through this exercise until you find the time period it occurred in.

Step Two—Determine Where You Lived

Once you have your year of birth, you can ask questions about the country you lived in. Go through the alphabet, asking if your country of birth began with an *A,* a *B,* and so on. Naturally, if you have a hunch that you were born in a certain place, you can immediately ask your angle rods if this was the case.

Step Three—Work Out Your Name

It is easy to determine your sex in this past lifetime. Learning your name is much harder. I usually go through the alphabet again, asking if the first letter of my name was an *A,* and so on.

Step Four—Work Out Your Occupation

You can determine your occupation in the same way as the last few steps. However, I normally start out by asking about different types of occupations in the hope of saving time. I ask if I was involved in agriculture, teaching, medicine, music, and so on, asking about occupations that I already know I experienced in other lifetimes.

Step Five—Important People in Your Past Life

I also save time by asking if important people in this lifetime were with me in this past life. The people I inquire about are my parents, wife, children, and a handful of close relatives and friends.

Step Six—Marital Status and Family

I will then go on to ask questions about my marital status, whether or not I had children, was I rich or poor, healthy or ill, and so on. Naturally, I will also find out when I died.

Obviously, divining a past life in this manner is a slow, painstaking business without the immediacy or excitement of a hypnotic regression. However, dowsing works extremely well with other methods, and it enables you to learn all sorts of details that you might forget to ask, or not even think about, in the course of a hypnotic regression. For instance, dowsing is extremely good at providing specific dates and places. This is vital information if you intend on following up the regression with more research. Details such as these do not always come through in other types of regressions.

Pendulums

Although I use angle rods on occasion, I personally prefer to use a pendulum when dowsing for past lives. There are several reasons for this. A pendulum is simply a small weight attached to a chain or length of thread. Consequently, it is more convenient than angle rods. But more importantly, you can ask a much wider range of questions as you are not limited to simple "yes" and "no" answers. This speeds up the process.

The most famous pendulum dowser of all time was a French priest, Abbé Alexis Mermet. He used his pendulum mainly to diagnose and heal illnesses, but he also used it for many other purposes. From his office in Saint-Prex near Geneva, he was able to locate the positions of unexploded German shells that remained buried in French soil after World War I. He also located water for a school in Colombia, South America. After water was found exactly where he said it would be, the rector wrote back to Abbé Mermet to thank him, and to ask if he could dowse to see if there was any petroleum or valuable minerals on the property. On one occasion, Abbé Mermet located a missing cow and was able to tell the amazed farmer that the cow had fallen into a precipice one hundred meters deep. He also said that the cow would be lying with all four legs in the air. This proved to be the case.[3] Abbé Mermet was also famous for finding missing people. In May 1935 his work was recognized by the Vatican.

Your pendulum can be almost anything that can be suspended. I have used a paperclip attached to a piece of string when nothing else was available. The ideal weight is about three or four ounces. If the weight is too heavy, your arm will tire quickly. The best weights are round or symmetrical. Over the years I have built up a huge collection of novelty items that can be used as pendulums. My children joke that I need to dowse for the right pendulum for any particular task.

Hold the string of the pendulum between your thumb and first finger of your right hand if you are right-handed. If you are left-handed, use your left hand. Rest your elbow on a table, and allow the weight to swing freely an inch or so above the table's surface.

Stop the movement of the pendulum with your free hand. Once it has ceased moving, ask it to indicate what answer it will give for "yes." There are four possible movements. It might swing forward and backward, moving away from you and then back again. It may swing from side to side. It might decide to move in a circular motion, and this can be either clockwise or counterclockwise.

Once you have determined the "yes" direction, ask the pendulum to indicate "no." Then, there are still two directions available. Ask the pendulum to indicate "I don't know" and "I don't want to answer."

The pendulum movements that you receive to indicate the four replies may not be the same as mine.

They are unique to you. However, over time they may change. Consequently, it pays to ask these questions every now and again to make sure that your pendulum has not changed its mind.

Once you have ascertained the movements, confirm them by asking the pendulum the same questions that you asked the angle rods. Only then should you start asking the pendulum questions about your previous lives.

Denise's Experience

Denise has just completed her sophomore year at college. She intends to become a teacher, carrying on a family tradition as both of her parents are in the teaching profession.

She came to me just before Christmas to have a past-life regression. She was an excellent subject and had no problems in returning to a past life as a private tutor for the children of a wealthy man in Victorian England. However, despite being well educated and well read in this past life, Denise was unable to provide details of exactly whereabout in England the manor house was, or which family she worked for.

Using a pendulum, we discovered that she worked for a Sir William Williams and his family from 1850–1854. This gentleman's name seemed rather unusual, but the pendulum confirmed that it was correct. The pendulum also told us that the house was in Cornwall and had been built only a few years before Denise came to work for the family.

When Denise finishes her studies, she intends to visit Cornwall to learn more. Denise learned a great deal more by using her pendulum, but most of it was of a personal nature.

This is a typical example of how dowsing was able to amplify and enlarge upon the information provided by a regression.

11

Rainbow Number Meditation

The rainbow comes and goes,
And lovely is the rose,
The moon doth with delight
Look round her when the heavens are bare,
Waters on a starry night
Are beautiful and fair;
The sunshine is a glorious birth;
But yet I know, where'er I go,
That there hath passed away a glory from the earth.

William Wordsworth (1770–1850)

This interesting method of returning to your past lives can be done on your own or with a partner who can guide you through the experience. It is an extremely pleasant way of discovering past lives. However, it does have two disadvantages. This method usually produces small glimpses of many previous lives, rather than a detailed overview of one. This makes it impossible to verify the incidents afterward. The other disadvantage is that you have no control as to which past lives you will be returning to.

The rainbow number meditation method uses a progressive relaxation technique to ensure that you are physically relaxed. You then imagine yourself walking through a large, beautiful rainbow, experiencing the sensations of each color. Many people start gaining insights into past lives while still inside the rainbow. Once you are through the rainbow, you think of single- or double-digit numbers at random, and see what images come back to you.

For example, you might think of the number eight. While picturing this symbol in your mind, an image of one of your past lives may return to you. Enjoy the experience, and then think of another number. If you want to move forward in this incarnation, choose a number one or two higher than the original one. Usually this will take you to a later date in the incarnation you are exploring. However, it may also take you to a completely different lifetime. Naturally, if you want to ensure that you will experience a different life, think of a number well away from the first one.

So in a short space of time you can gain memories of dozens of previous lives. It is unlikely that you will obtain any verifiable details as you will only experience brief glimpses. However, you may see people who are important to you in this lifetime in some of your past lives. You may find that you followed similar careers in many previous existences. You may also gain insights into the type of person you were each time.

I usually use this method to uncover past lives that I am not already familiar with. Once I have discovered them in this way, I can then explore them in greater detail using one of the other methods. I find this to be one of the most enjoyable methods of returning to past lifetimes.

If you wish, you can record the script below on tape and follow it through. The disadvantage of this is that your voice on the tape might force you to move ahead while you are experiencing a particularly vivid past life. In practice, I become familiar with the basic ideas in the script and then say it to myself in my own words. This means that I can lead myself through the experiment at my own pace.

The other alternative is to do this exercise with a partner. Before you start, arrange a simple signal so that the person going through the exercise can instruct the person reading the script to move forward again. The easiest signal is a small movement of the thumb. This does not affect the person being regressed, and it allows the other person to know what is going on.

Rainbow Number Meditation

Step One—Progressive Relaxation

Sit or lie down in a comfortable position. Ensure that the room is reasonably warm and that you will not be interrupted. You might want to cover yourself with a blanket, as you will lose one or two degrees of body temperature during this meditation.

Take a nice deep breath in, and then close your eyes as you exhale. Become aware of your breathing, and allow yourself to relax more and more with each easy breath you take. It's a pleasant feeling to simply relax and let the world carry on without you for a short while. Each breath makes you more and more relaxed, more and more relaxed.

Focus on your toes now, and allow them to relax. When you feel that they are relaxed, allow the relaxation to flow into your feet until both feet are totally limp and relaxed. Allow the pleasant relax-

ation to drift into your ankles, and then gradually move up your legs, into your calf muscles, knees, and thighs. Just relaxing more and more with each breath you take. Nothing need bother or disturb you as you continue to relax, deeper, and deeper, and deeper.

Feel that pleasant relaxation drifting into your abdomen now, and up and into your stomach. The whole lower half of your body is so, so relaxed now, limp, loose, and so completely relaxed.

Allow the relaxation to drift up into your chest and into your shoulders. Feel the relaxation spreading over and into your shoulders, taking away all the stress, tension, and tightness. When your shoulders feel completely relaxed, allow the relaxation to drift down each arm to the tips of your fingers.

Turn your attention to your neck, and allow all the muscles in your neck to relax. Feel the relaxation steadily drifting up and into your face, and right up to the top of your head. Allow the muscles around your eyes to relax.

Take a deep breath in and exhale slowly. You feel totally relaxed now, from the top of your head to the tips of your toes, and each breath you take allows you to go even deeper into this pleasant state of total relaxation and tranquillity.

Mentally scan your body now, and see if every area is as relaxed as you'd like it to be. Focus on any places that still feel tight or tense and allow the muscles to relax, until finally, you are totally, completely, absolutely limp, loose, and relaxed.

Step Two—Through the Rainbow

In this nice, pleasant state of total relaxation, visualize yourself out in the country. You are walking over a field of lush, fresh grass. It's a gorgeous day, and the sky is a radiant blue with just a few fluffy clouds high up in the sky.

Ahead of you is a magnificent, perfect rainbow. You feel excited as you have never been this close to the foot of a rainbow before. It smells fresh and clean, and the colors are more vibrant that anything you've ever experienced before.

You walk right up to the rainbow until you are standing so close that you could touch it. When you look up, the rainbow appears to go straight up into the sky. You reach out to touch the rainbow, and your hand goes right through and into the red area. Your hand feels slightly tingly, and you realize that the red is making your hand and arm relax even more.

It feels so good, that you decide to step inside the rainbow. When you look around now, all you can see is red. Red in front of you, behind you, on each side, and above and below you. You are totally bathed and encircled by this gorgeous red.

It feels so pure, so restful, so quiet, and yet so comforting. All you can think of is red, red, red. . . .

Pause for about sixty seconds. Many people spontaneously experience a past life at this point. If this happens to you, enjoy it for as long as you wish, and then continue with the meditation. If you do not return to a past life, wait sixty seconds, and then carry on.

You feel like moving on now, so you take a few steps forward, and now you have entered the orange area. The red felt so comforting and relaxing, but that was nothing compared to the utter tranquillity and peace of the orange. You feel the gentle orange permeating every cell of your body. You are totally surrounded by orange, and you are also part of the orange as it is inside every cell of your body. You are nothing but pure orange, orange, orange. . . .

Pause for sixty seconds, and see if you receive memories of one of your past lives. If you do, enjoy them for as long as you wish, and then continue. If nothing comes through, continue after sixty seconds.

The desire to explore further comes to your awareness, and you take another few steps forward until you are in the yellow section. You are familiar with the color yellow, but you have never experienced a color as perfect and serene as this one. You feel as if you'd like to enjoy being bathed in its energies forever, as it is so peaceful, tranquil, and perfect. Surrounded by pure yellow, yellow, yellow. . . .

Again pause for sixty seconds and see what happens. When you are ready, continue with the meditation.

And you are now ready to walk through into the green. The vibrant, healing energy of the green almost takes your breath away. You feel restored and invigorated in every pore of your being. Relax and allow the green to move into every cell of your body. Oh, this beautiful green, green, green. . . .

Pause for sixty seconds, and continue when ready.

It's only a few steps until you're completely surrounded by blue. You've seen beautiful blues before, but nothing to compare with the majesty of this. You look around, entranced by the wonder of this gorgeous blue, blue, blue. . . .

Again, pause for sixty seconds.

And now you're moving into the healing energies of indigo. You feel better than you've ever felt before, and you're enjoying the feelings of deep peace and contentment as you gaze around at the magnificent indigo, indigo, indigo. . . .

Pause again for sixty seconds.

There's only one color left to visit. You're anxious to move on to violet, but you retain all the feelings you felt while experiencing the wonderful qualities of the other colors.

And now it's time to move on. One step, two steps, and three. You are now surrounded by the spiritual qualities of violet. You feel it spreading into every organ of your body, restoring your body, mind, and soul. You feel as if you could stay inside the violet for ever, enjoying it's soothing tenderness and gentle awakening of your spiritual center. There's something indescribable about violet, violet, violet. . . .

Pause again for sixty seconds. By this stage you may already have experienced a number of past lives.

Alternatively, you may not have experienced any yet. This does not matter, because the next stage is designed to unlock your long-forgotten memories of previous incarnations.

Step Three—Past Life After Past Life

And now it is time to leave the rainbow behind. You are reluctant to leave, but you know that the rainbow meditation is just a foretaste of what is to come. So now you step out of the rainbow, and back onto the luscious grass of the field. You find a nice, pleasant spot to lie down in, you take a long deep breath in, and you let it out slowly.

You are now totally relaxed in every nerve, fiber, and cell of your being. You are limp, loose, and so, so relaxed. You have experienced the nurturing energies of each color of the rainbow, and now you are ready to return to one of your past lives.

Without considering the matter first, simply think of a number, any number. As you think about this number, memories will come back you, memories of one of your many past lives.

From here on, you can progress in any way you wish. If the first number you think of takes you back to an interesting past life, explore it for as long as you want. You might be able to move backward and forward in this lifetime by thinking of numbers close to your original number. Once you have gained everything you want from this lifetime, you can choose another number and see what comes into your mind. You can do this for as short or long a period as you want, finally returning to the present when you feel ready.

Step Four—Back to the Present

And now it is time to let go of these experiences and return to the present. These memories will not be lost. You will remember them all when you return to your everyday life. You will also be able to explore them in greater detail whenever you wish.

So now you are returning to the present, moving back through time and space until you are back where you were at the start. In your mind's eye, see yourself inside the room you are in. Picture the surroundings, the furniture, and become aware of any sounds outside the room.

And now, on the count of five, you'll open your eyes feeling refreshed, invigorated, and with full recall of everything that happened during this regression.

One, coming up now, feeling happy and full of energy.

Two, feeling wonderful, perfect in every way.

Three, feeling as if you've had a wonderful night's sleep.

Four, ready to face the world again.

And five, eyes opening, full of energy and feeling great.

Naturally, if you are doing this experiment in bed at night, you would not want to wake up at the end. In this case, after returning to the present, you simply tell yourself that you will fall fast asleep, sleeping soundly all night long, until it is time to wake up in the morning.

I prefer not to do this experiment in bed. I find that if I do, I become so relaxed that I usually fall asleep before I've made my way through the rainbow. I have noticed that I experience particularly vivid dreams when I fall asleep this way. However, they are not usually connected with my previous lives.

Sometimes you will uncover dozens of past lives in a short space of time. When I use this method, I write down everything I can remember as soon as possible after conducting this experiment. I may ignore some lives that did not interest me very much, but I always take detailed notes of the others while the incidents are still fresh in my mind.

Jeremy's Experience

Jeremy is a twenty-six-year-old computer programmer. He loves mathematics and came to my classes after reading *Numerology Magic,* a book I wrote about magic square yantras. He was intrigued to learn that there was more to numbers than he had thought.

He found it hard to relax initially. By the time he had gone all the way through the rainbow, he was still not completely relaxed and stopped at that point. The second time he went through the relaxation process twice before entering the rainbow. This time he felt the colors much more vividly than before, and moved on to the next stage.

The first number he chose was seven. This was because we had previously discussed the spiritual significance of this number in class. Nothing came to him, and he opened his eyes.

He made a third attempt a few days later. As he was going through the rainbow he caught a glimpse of himself paddling a canoe down what appeared to be a canal. He had never done that in real life, and was so surprised that he almost opened his eyes. Fortunately, he continued, this time with much more confidence than before.

When it was time to think of a number, he again chose seven. I would have suggested that he start with a different number, but obviously the number seven struck a special chord in his mind. This time he got a faint impression of a family scene. It was somewhere in southeast Asia, and a man, woman, and two children were sitting on a bamboo porch. Somehow he realized that he was the woman in the scene.

No further information came, so he thought of the number eight, thinking that it might take him to another scene in the same life. This time he found himself under a bed while a couple made love above him. He was horrified to think that he might have been having an affair with the woman, and suddenly realized that neither of them knew he was there. He was a burglar.

He wanted to get away from that lifetime as quickly as possible, so he thought of the number eighty-seven. He was instantly transported to a small, cramped office in Victorian times. He was sitting on a high stool and was poring over figures in an account book.

"I want a lifetime away from mathematics," he thought, and without thinking of another number he found himself as an actor in Roman times. Unfortunately, the audience did not like the role he was playing, and he was booed loudly every time he went on stage. "I tried to explain that I was only acting," Jeremy told me, "but they booed all the more." He quickly thought of another number.

This time he was a peasant somewhere in central Asia. "The land was flat, and spread out endlessly in every direction. It was cold most of the time, and we lived on stew. The only fun we had was getting drunk."

Jeremy thought of another number and found himself in Georgian London. His son in that life was his father in his present life, but he could not identify anyone else. "We had nothing in common," he said. "It's sad, really, as in this life we have nothing in common either." Jeremy made a mental note to explore that final life in more detail, because there was obviously a karmic factor between him and his father, and then returned to the present.

Despite the sadness of some of the lives, Jeremy was ecstatic. "I can't remember ever having more fun on my own," he told me.

12

Imagination
Meditation

*Our deeds still travel with us from afar, and what
we have been makes us what we are.*

George Eliot (1818–1880)

T his method was an extremely useful one
in my classes, particularly for people
who failed to regress using any other method.
I began using it so that these people would
have a taste of what a regression felt like. To
my surprise, most of these people began with

an imaginary scene but then moved on to an actual past life.

I am not sure why this should be the case. Perhaps these people had a subconscious fear about letting go and returning to a past life. Once they discovered how enjoyable the process was, they lost this fear, and were able to effortlessly move back to a previous existence. Perhaps the imaginary experience caused them to remember certain incidents that brought back past-life memories.

However, the reasons do not matter. What is important is that the imagination meditation works extremely well, and enables many people to rediscover their past lives.

Imagination Meditation

Step One—The Time and the Setting

Spend some time thinking about periods of history that particularly interest you. It might be during the French Revolution. Perhaps Imperial Rome intrigues you. Maybe a lifetime in Atlantis. Some people deliberately choose a time of excitement, while others prefer a period of peace.

You might choose the time and place when a particular hero of yours was alive. If you are interested in drama, you might choose the London that William Shakespeare lived and worked in. You might decide to live in the Europe of Nostradamus. You might like to be on the small ship that Christopher Columbus crossed the Atlantic in. It makes no difference what time or place you choose, just as long as it appeals to you.

The time and place may have no bearing on your past lives. It is simply a starting point for the meditation. All the same, it is amazing how often people choose a time that interests them, and then find themselves experiencing a past life in that period. No doubt this explains why they were interested in that particular period of history.

Step Two—Progressive Relaxation

Choose a time when you are not likely to be disturbed. Make yourself as comfortable as possible and then go through a progressive relaxation to ensure that you are completely relaxed. You might choose to do the first two stages of the rainbow number meditation in chapter 11. If you have learned how to meditate, you might choose to start off with a meditation. Alternatively, you might decide to first tense and then relax all of the muscles in your body, starting with your toes and gradually working your way up through your body. It does not matter which method you use, just as long as you feel totally relaxed at the end of it.

Step Three—Imaginary Past Life

Once you are completely relaxed, inhale deeply and exhale slowly. Tell yourself that you are going to move back through time and space to the period you decided on in step one.

Once you are there, visualize the scene as clearly as possible. People experience things in different ways. There is no need to worry if you do not see it as clearly as you would like. Some people see it so clearly that they would swear that they were inside the scene. Other people see very little, but experience it in other ways. They might feel the scene, or be unusually aware of all the sounds and smells.

Once you become familiar with the scene you are in, you can move backward or forward through time. You can see yourself at home, at work, or at play.

There is no need to hurry. Spend several minutes exploring the period in history that you chose. You will find it a fascinating experience, and will feel as if you are actually living in that time and place.

Step Four—Return to a Valid Past Life

Step three serves two purposes. First, it allows you to experience the sights, sounds, tastes, and other experiences of a period in history. In other words, it is virtually the same as a real past life. This prepares you for the real past-life experiences to come. Second, it enables you to relax even further.

Take another deep breath in and exhale slowly. With your eyes closed, visualize yourself as you are, sitting or lying down. In your mind's eye see the scene as clearly as you can.

Once you can see yourself in your imagination, picture a bank of fog gradually sweeping over you until you are completely enveloped in fog. Wait until the scene in your mind is a swirling mass of white fog and you can no longer see yourself.

Take a long deep breath in and let it out as slowly as you can, at the same time allowing the fog to slowly move away. As the fog disappears, you will no longer see yourself sitting or lying down quietly. Instead you will be inside a scene from one of your past lives.

Allow a minute or two to become familiar with the scene you find yourself within. Experience it in as many different ways as you can. Look around and see it, feel it, smell it, and even taste it. When you are ready, move forward or backward in this past life, and explore it in as much detail as you wish.

Remember to visit scenes that reveal who you loved the most in that lifetime, what you did for a living, how you spent your time, what lessons needed to be learned, and what karma was created and paid back.

Some scenes will be happy, while others might be neutral or painful. You can move back from the painful ones and observe them from a distance. You can move completely away if you wish, but it is better to learn the bad aspects of your previous lives as well as the good.

Step Five—Return to the Present

When you have learned all that you need to know in this session, return to the present by counting silently from one to five. Remain quiet with your eyes closed for a minute or so, and then count up to five again and open your eyes.

Now that you have experienced a valid past life, you will be able to return to it again whenever you wish. However, that may not be necessary. Memories will flow into your conscious mind over the next few days now that the memories have been unlocked.

If you have not been able to return to your past lives using the other methods, you will find that this will cease to be a problem, now that you have succeeded using this method. Some people prefer to continue using this method, but others like to experiment with other ways of returning to explore their past lives. I enjoy experimenting with different techniques, but it is not necessary. All you need is one method that works for you.

Maria's Experience

Maria is a twenty-eight-year-old physiotherapist. She wants to write romance novels, and once she mastered the imagination meditation technique, she began using the first two stages to help plot her stories.

"I was probably overkeen to return to my past lives," she told me. "I'd read about Joan Grant and how her novels were basically memories of her past lives and thought I'd like to do the same. I was anxious and stressed, and that probably made it impossible for me to go back using the other methods. This method was a brilliant one for me. I was used to imagining scenes for my writing, and when you asked me to choose a time and period, I didn't have to stop and think. I knew I wanted to go back to Regency England.

"Well, everything was so clear to me in my mind. I'd researched the period, of course, and this made me nervous. I started imagining scenes—a party in an exclusive house in London, shopping in the Burlington Arcade, things like that. I thought the clarity was because I'd already read so much about it. I found out later that the scenes were always that clear to me. It was easy to imagine myself surrounded by fog too.

"I thought it wasn't going to happen when the fog started to move away. I saw nothing, nothing at all, but I could feel movement. And then I realized I was swimming and had my eyes closed. Once I discovered that, the water began to get cold and I opened my eyes and headed for shore. It was almost dark and the beach was pebbly. There was no one there except for me. I knew where my clothes and towel were, so I found them and started to dry myself. That's when I realized I was naked. I suddenly felt vulnerable and afraid. I dressed quickly and headed home. I knew exactly where to go, and once I started walking I felt safe again. We—my dad and I—lived in a small cottage with a thatched roof. I could see and smell the smoke coming out of the chimney as I approached.

"I could smell a stew cooking when I opened the door, and remembered that Dad had caught a rabbit that morning. Supper was all ready, and Dad smiled when I came in. It wasn't my dad in this lifetime. I don't know who he was, but I knew I loved him and that he was my dad. He cared for me, and worried about me all the time. He didn't want me to leave. But I had to, as I was engaged to be married."

Maria laughed. "My fiancé is my younger brother in this lifetime. I sort of wanted to laugh when he came in, but I didn't, of course, as it felt right. I've always been extremely close to my little brother, and now I know why. He's the only person from my present life that I could identify in this life.

"I wanted to marry, to get away from this little village and the country life. Some hope! I was uneducated, illiterate, and Sean was too. Only he wasn't Sean, he was William. He was a farm laborer. He promised me the moon, and he meant it too, but there was no way we could better ourselves.

"We had a nice wedding. Everyone was there. No honeymoon, of course. We spent our first night in a shack behind our cottage. It was meant to be only for the night, but it was years before we could move out. We had three little ones by then.

"It was a good life, a happy life, but it was marred because I was never satisfied. I always wanted more. Sean—William—did the best he could, but we were always short of money. I never went anywhere. I was old when I died, and I'd still never been more than a couple of miles in any direction."

"Were you full of regrets when you died?"

Maria nodded. "I had so many regrets. Regrets that I'd never been anywhere, regrets that I hadn't been to see my dad for days before he died, regrets that I didn't give my children a better start. But my main regret was that I'd made William's life so miserable. No matter what he did for me, it was never enough. I wanted more, more, more. He promised to take me to London, but of course we didn't go. I held that against him always. And then he died, and I couldn't say sorry. I was a miserable old cow!" She frowned. "I spoil Sean. I guess I'm trying to make up for what I did to him then."

"Was this lifetime in the Regency period?"

Maria laughed. "Ironic, isn't it? Yes, I was alive at the right time, but my life was completely different from that of the wealthy, beautiful people in London—the people I want to write about."

Maria took herself back to this lifetime several times and uncovered a great deal of information. She now plans to write a novel based on it.

"The memories are so vivid, they could have happened yesterday. In fact, they're just as strong as any memories I have of this life. I'm going to write a romance novel, but it will really be an autobiography!"

Maria has not yet had time to experiment with the other methods of retracing her past lives. Neither has she explored any other lifetimes.

"There'll be time for that later," she told me. "Right now I'm too busy trying to find every last detail of that life. I want the book to be as accurate as possible."

It would be interesting to know how many historical novels are actually memories of previous lifetimes. Joan Grant claimed that many of her books were transcriptions of her earlier lives. Many years ago, I read a book titled *Echo* by Shaw Desmond. I did not realize until I read another book of his, *Reincarnation for Everyman,* that *Echo* was an account of his lifetime in Rome at the time of Nero.[1] There must be many other examples.

13

Exploring the Akashic Records

The collective unconscious is common to all; it is the foundation of what the ancients called the "sympathy of all things."

Carl Jung (1875–1961)

The Akashic records is a storehouse containing complete records on everything that has ever happened in the universe. Every thought, feeling, or action is stored away there, and can be accessed on request. It is a collective memory that all of us can tap into when we need information. In effect, it contains not only everyone's personal records, but also the records of every family, tribe, and country. It has been described as being an "incredible psychic computer."[1]

The medieval Islamic philosopher Averroes (1128–1198) wrote that although we have separate bodies, we do not possess separate minds. He believed that we are "like an aquatic plant with many heads showing above water, but all meeting in one great root beneath the surface."[2]

The Akashic records can be compared to Jung's theory of the collective unconscious. Carl Jung coined this term to represent the entire thought-substance of the human race.

Edgar Cayce described the Akashic records as a giant library. In a talk he gave at the Cayce Hospital in 1931 he explained how he left his body, traveled down a shaft of light, and ultimately came to a hill containing a temple. "I entered this temple," he said, "and found in it a very large room, very much like a library. Here were the books of people's lives, for each person's activities were a matter of actual record, it seemed. And I merely had to pull down the record of the individual for whom I was seeking information."[3]

The Akashic records contain information on all of your previous lives, as well as clues to your probable future lives. It takes practice to get there, but once you have succeeded, it is not difficult to examine the Akashic records of your own lives whenever you wish. It is a great deal harder to examine the Akashic records of other people. However, it can be done with practice, and many people, such as clairvoyants, do it on a regular basis.

When you view your own Akashic records you will find your hopes and dreams for each life you have led. You will also learn how you acted and behaved. You will discover what motivated you and what held you back at each stage.

Akashic Record Meditation

Step One—Get in Tune

Spend some time thinking about your need to view your Akashic records. You need the right reasons to go there. It is unlikely that you will be successful if you are motivated simply by curiosity, for instance. If your motivation is to learn something about your past that will enable you to act better in the future, you will undoubtedly succeed. Likewise if you are wanting to develop spiritually or mentally. Visiting the Akashic records is not a party trick or something that is done purely for fun. It is a serious quest, and you need to approach it in the right frame of mind.

Step Two—Relaxation

Once you have your reasons for visiting the Akashic records clear in your mind, you can progress to the next step. Find a comfortable spot where you will not be disturbed for an hour or so. Relax using any method that you are comfortable with. I use a progressive relaxation, but tensing and then relaxing, meditation, or any other method that allows you to temporarily forget about the cares of the day will work just as well.

Step Three—Leave the Body

Mentally scan your body to make sure that you are totally relaxed. Focus on any remaining areas of tension until you are certain that you are completely loose, limp, and relaxed in every cell of your body.

Think about your need to visit the Akashic records. Then imagine that your spirit or soul is loosening its hold on your body and is gradually floating up and away from you. Place your center of awareness in your spirit and you'll be able to see yourself, relaxed and peaceful. Mentally send protection to your physical body to keep it safe while you are away.

Step Four—Approach the Akashic Records

Once you have become familiar with the situation you are in you can allow your spirit to flow free through time and space until it reaches the Akashic records.

Visualize your soul hurtling through a long tunnel and then coming out into fresh, clear air high up in the sky. Below you you see a small, perfectly formed hill with a white temple on top. As you descend, you notice that the green grass has been freshly mown. It looks soft and fluffy. The green grass harmonizes well with the crisp, clean, white marble of the temple.

You land in a courtyard in front of the main entrance to the temple. A large man is standing there, and you realize that he is the doorkeeper to the temple.

Step Five—Ask For What You Want

Although you are in spirit form, the doorkeeper welcomes you with a low bow and a smile. He waits for you to tell him what you want. You tell him your name and say that you would like to view your book.

He asks you to wait for a moment. He goes inside and then returns almost immediately. He holds the door open so that you can enter.

You come into a large room that is like a huge library, full of rows and rows of books. You notice that many of the records are books, but others are in the form of scrolls and tablets.

The doorkeeper ushers you into a small room containing a large table and a chair. Sitting on the table is your record. The room is warm and comfortable. There appears to be no light source, but the room is evenly lit throughout. You feel at peace in this room.

The doorkeeper bows again and then leaves you alone, softly closing the door behind him.

Step Six—Explore Your Record

You spend a few moments simply looking at your record. It is hard to believe that the entire record of all your thoughts and actions, conscious and subconscious, over all of your lifetimes, is contained in this book.

You know it is your record, as it speaks to you, telepathically imparting everything that you wish to know. You can open the book if you wish. Alternatively, you can simply allow the information to flow effortlessly into your mind.

You will absorb the information in many ways. Some will come as a sense of understanding and knowing. Other material will be re-enacted in front of you, just as it occurred so long before. Other information, particularly errors, misjudgments, and mistakes, will appear like clothes on a long clothesline. The clothesline represents the thread that connects all of your many lifetimes, and the clothes depict mistakes you have made along the way. These all need to be made right before you can progress further. They are all karmic factors that need to be attended to.

Some of your past lives will be in magnificent colors, reflecting the glories and successes you had in those incarnations. Other lives will be in pastel colors, showing that you enjoyed a pleasant lifetime but did not achieve more than a fraction of what you were capable of doing. Still other lives will be in black and white. These were negative lifetimes. You may or may not have been a bad person in these lives, but you failed to pay back many karmic debts and accumulated more as a result of these incarnations.

You will become aware of themes that flow through many lifetimes. You will understand where your particular talents came from, and you will realize how much further you can develop these skills. You will see how certain people follow you from lifetime to lifetime. You will notice how the relationships change so that everyone experiences every possible combination.

You will learn where your fears and phobias came from. Once you understand the reasons behind them, they will cease to have any relevance in your current life.

You will also discover how your thoughts and actions in this lifetime are affecting your future lives virtually on a daily basis. You will understand what is important and what is not important in this incarnation.

You can stay in this beautiful room for as long as you wish. You may find that you want to return as soon as you have the information you need. Alternatively, you might decide to stay longer simply to enjoy being with all of your past lives and understand the connection among them all.

Step Seven—Return to the Present

When you are ready, all you need to do is think that it is time to return. The doorkeeper will immediately open the door and escort you out to the courtyard. He will bow solemnly and tell you that you are welcome to visit whenever you wish.

You will feel a sudden pull, and instantly you'll be back in your physical body. Usually the return is smooth and effortless. Occasionally you may feel a sudden jerking motion as you return.

Remain sitting quietly for a minute or so before opening your eyes and returning to your everyday world. You will experience a glow of satisfaction and a sense of incredible well-being when you open your eyes. You will also be motivated to make the very best of yourself in the future.

You will have gained enormous insight into many of your past lives, and you will have the reassuring knowledge that you can return to the Akashic records any time you wish.

Conrad's Experience

Conrad is a forty-four-year-old accountant. It would be hard to find anyone more down-to-earth and rational. He freely admits that he came to my classes originally because his wife did not want to come on her own. However, she lost interest quickly, but he carried on. He had no problems in returning to his past lives, but he liked the Akashic record method best.

"It appeals to my logical mind," he says. "I can go to one place—the Akashic records—and see all of my past lives at one time. I need examine only the ones I want to see at that particular time. What I really like is that I can get a clear overview of my life's purpose over thousands of years. I got that to an extent when I was dowsing my past lives, but I never got to meet anyone exciting like the doorkeeper. I find it so fantastic that I can communicate with him telepathically. He seems to read my thoughts at the same time as I receive them, even faster sometimes. I think of something, and immediately he attends to it."

Conrad has been a male in almost all of the incarnations he has looked at. After examining perhaps one hundred lives, he has been female in only three.

"I don't know why I'm usually a male," he says. "I'm not a macho man or sexist in any way. It's just the way it's happened with me. It seems that in my female lives

I needed the female perspective to learn the lessons that I had to learn in those incarnations."

In most of his lives he has been an intellectual. He has been a monk, a teacher, a researcher, and an artist. He relates strongly to all of these themes in his present life. Many of his previous lives involve dealings with money, and he has been a bookkeeper and an accountant several times. "I hope I'm doing something a bit more exciting next time," he laughs. "I'm getting tired of always being an accountant."

The lifetime that intrigues him most, though, was when he was a landowner in South Africa in the middle of the nineteenth century. In that lifetime he was particularly brutal to his workers.

"I can't understand that one," he told me. "In every other life I seem to have been a caring person, but for some strange reason, I was a monster in that incarnation. Why?"

There does not appear to be a logical answer to this. However, although he was cruel to his workers, his behavior was not considered unusual at the time. His lifetime immediately after that was spent as a Christian missionary in northwest Africa.

"There was no doubt that I was a dedicated missionary. Maybe I was atoning for the earlier life," Conrad muses. "It's strange, though. I consider myself a spiritual person, but I don't belong to any orthodox church. Yet I have a good knowledge of the Bible. I guess I must have learned much of that when I was a missionary."

Conrad feels that his love of order and detail comes across strongly in all of his lifetimes. "I'd hate to be called finicky," he says. "I definitely was in some of my earlier lives, but I think I've got that out of my system now. In this lifetime I'm working on taking life more as it comes. I used to worry all the time, usually about silly things. That's much more under control now. And that is due to the Akashic records. If I hadn't seen these traits passing on from one life to the next, I wouldn't have been so aware of them. It's made a big difference to my life, and my family has noticed how much more relaxed I am now too."

Conrad is continuing to explore his past lives using a variety of methods. He and his family have noticed an improvement in every aspect of his life since becoming aware of his previous incarnations.

14

The Feeling Technique

The only survival I can conceive is to start a new earth cycle again.

Thomas Edison (1847–1931)

This technique is not a good one for everyone, as it involves following your fears, hurts, traumas, and phobias all the way back to their source in a previous life.

We bring into this lifetime a surprising amount of baggage from the past. Obviously, someone born with abnormal fears must have learned about them in a past life. If he or she had never encountered that particular situation before, there would be no need for the dread or fear.

My older son was born with a fear of deep water and found it extremely hard to learn to swim. His younger brother was the complete opposite and loved playing in our swimming pool from an early age. Obviously, my older son experienced something extremely traumatic relating to water in one of his past lives, and was born this time with strong fears about it.

One of my clients had a strong fear of snakes, and moved to New Zealand in her early twenties to get away from them. However, the fear remained even while living in a country that has no snakes. She found it impossible to enjoy a picnic in the woods or a walk in the country because she felt it was possible that someone may have smuggled a snake in. Even knowing that this had never happened did nothing to assuage her fears.

I regressed her back to a past life in which she hid in a cave to avoid being raped. Just as she felt she was safe, she discovered she was sharing her hiding place with a large snake. The fear of the snake was worse than the terror outside, and she raced out of the cave to her death. After reliving the experience, she completely lost her fear of snakes. Proudly displayed in her living room is a photograph of herself taken at the Singapore Zoo. Draped around her shoulders is a large python.

The fear of insects, rats, mice, and snakes is very common and often relates to past incarnations in the Middle Ages when rats and mice were the cause of the plague.

One of my clients had an intense fear of enclosed spaces. In a past life he was a Catholic priest who was forced to hide in a small cupboard while King Henry VIII's soldiers searched the house. He was unconscious by the time the soldiers left, and has had a fear of confined spaces ever since.

Whatever it is that you fear has an annoying tendency to repeat itself over and over again until you have dealt with it. The feeling technique is not just an effective way of returning to a past life, you can also use the regression to release trauma created during past lifetimes. The technique is simple and straightforward.

The Feeling Technique
Step One—Relaxation
Sit down somewhere where you feel safe and protected. This is likely to be somewhere at home. It is better to do this particular regression indoors as you want to feel protected and secure throughout.

Make yourself as comfortable as possible. Ensure that the room is warm enough and that you will not be disturbed for an hour or so.

Close your eyes and take three deep breaths, holding each one for a moment or two, and then exhaling slowly.

Think about something pleasant that you have done recently. This can be anything at all, but it is important that it is a time when you enjoyed yourself and had no underlying worries or concerns.

After thinking about the pleasant experience for a while, allow your mind to drift and think about other pleasant occasions you have enjoyed in the past.

Enjoy your thoughts for a few minutes, and then say silently to yourself, "I am completely relaxed and free of stress." Repeat these words over and over again. As you do this, you will find yourself relaxing more and more.

You can move on to the next stage when you feel that you are totally relaxed.

Body Awareness

Become aware of your body. In your mind's eye see yourself sitting or lying down in your room. Surround your body with a circle of protection. Imagine a cone of pure white light descending from the ceiling and surrounding your physical body. At the same time remind yourself that you are protected and safe.

Enjoy these sensations for a minute or two. Then when you feel ready, think about your fear or phobia. Feel it in your physical body. You may feel a heaviness or sense of discomfort or unease somewhere in your body. It might be a tightening in your chest, shortness of breath, or a headache. Usually the area will be related to the phobia. If you had a fear of fire, for instance, this sensation would possibly be a constriction in your nose and throat.

Allow the sensation in your body to build and grow. Give it a color. Once you have this color clear in your mind, give it a shape. It can be any shape you wish. Most people choose round, square, or triangular shapes, but you need not be restricted by these. Choose a shape that reflects the pain and discomfort. Notice that you can make this shape larger and smaller. As it grows larger, so does the sense of discomfort in your body. As it decreases in size, so does the discomfort. Experiment with making it larger and smaller. Finally, reduce it in size so that you can sense only a mild feeling of discomfort.

Step Three—Explore This Lifetime

Allow your mind to drift back to other occasions when you felt this discomfort or when you were aware of your fear or phobia. You are still in control of the shape and you can reduce it in size if any of the memories become too painful.

Take your time at this stage and see how many occasions in the past you can remember when you were affected by your fear or phobia.

Step Four—Previous Lifetimes

Take a deep breath in and exhale slowly. You are now going to enlarge the shape, which will increase the feelings of discomfort in your body. Allow the shape to grow as large as you can stand, and then allow yourself to go back to the very first time you ever felt this sensation.

It may take several seconds to locate the pivotal experience. Once you are there, allow the shape to get smaller and smaller, until it finally disappears.

You will now be in a past life. Look around and see where you are and what is happening. Remember that you are still surrounded by the ring of protection, and nothing can hurt you.

Watch the scene that is being played out and see what insights it gives into your fear or phobia. If it provides you with all the information that you need, you can let it go, confident that it will have no further effect upon you.

If you feel that this scene does not provide you with all the answers you need, allow the shape to grow in size again. Take a deep breath, and as you exhale, ask to be taken back to another pivotal experience that relates to your fear or phobia. You can repeat this as many times as you wish.

Usually people use this method of returning to their past lives to eliminate something that is holding them back in this lifetime. However, once you have regressed back to another life and resolved the difficulty, there is no reason why you should not move on and explore the lifetime in greater depth. There is much to be said for this. Increased knowledge of this past life will help you understand how the problem came about in the first place, and aid in letting it go.

Step Five—Back to the Present

Once you have explored this past life you can return to the present at any time by counting from one to five. Do not open your eyes immediately. Think about what you have learned and achieved with this regression. Realize that as a result your life will be easier, happier, and more fulfilled because you have eliminated something that was holding you back.

Become aware of the ring of protection surrounding you. Give thanks for what has been achieved and open your eyes.

Jeanette's Experience

Jeanette is eighteen and works as an office assistant. She is planning to go to college eventually, but at the moment she has no idea as to what she wants to do with her life. All her life she has had a fear of meeting strangers. She experiences a tightness in her chest, which makes it hard for her to breathe. She blushes and feels confused. She also finds it hard to look people in the eye. She had experienced difficulty in meeting new people all her life, but over the last few years the problem has gotten worse. She had taken a self-confidence course which helped temporarily, but came to me at her mother's insistence. I half expected her not to turn up for her appointment as I was yet another stranger, but she arrived a few minutes early, a nervous smile on her face.

She had no difficulty in imagining the feelings in her own body. She felt the tightness in her chest and blushed. She described the feeling as being black and almond-shaped. Jeanette was good at visualization and was able to make the almond smaller and larger without problems.

When I asked her to return to the very first time in which she had experienced these feelings she went back to a past life in primitive conditions. She and her family lived on the edge of a desert and were always struggling to survive. The temperatures were unbearably hot during the day, and dropped to zero at night. The family would huddle together for warmth.

One day her father commented on a large group of men riding across the desert toward them. Jeanette was about six at the time, and joined her father at the doorway of their hut to watch them approach. There were about twenty men in the group, all seated on camels. The leader of the group asked Jeanette's father for food and water. Her father was hospitable and offered them a small amount of water. However, he explained, he had nothing for them to eat.

The leader of the group was furious. He pointed at the three skinny goats the family owned and demanded that he kill one of them for him and his men. When Jeanette's father refused, the man got off his camel and stabbed him in the heart. The men took the three goats and rode away. Jeanette was kneeling down beside her dead father when her heavily pregnant mother and the other three children came out of the hut.

None of them cried. Instinctively, Jeanette knew that they were all going to die as they had lost both the breadwinner of the family and their wealth in the space of a few minutes. The children were too young to bury their father. They dragged him out into the desert and left him there. Then they returned home and waited to die. It didn't take long.

Jeanette told the story in a halting monotone. When she reached the part about not being able to bury her father she burst into tears and cried for several minutes.

She nodded when I asked her if this sad story accounted for her fear of strangers.

"Are you able to let it go now?" I asked. "Do you realize that most people are basically good?"

She nodded again. "It's gone," she said. "I've let it go."

Jeanette looked completely different when she returned to the present. She had more life and energy and was able to look me straight in the eyes.

Several days later her mother called to thank me for transforming her daughter's life.

"It's as if she's starting life all over again," she said. "She never stops talking and laughing. She even had a boy phone her last night. That's never happened before."

15

With the Help
of Your Guides

The soul of man is like to water;
  From Heaven it cometh
  To Heaven it riseth
And then returneth to earth. . . .

Johann Wolfgang von Goethe (1749–1832)

We all have invisible helpers who are prepared to offer us advice and counsel
whenever we need it. These are our guardian
angels and spirit guides. Spirit guides are people

who have died and moved on. However, they still retain an interest in what is happening in this lifetime, and are available to give help whenever the person they are looking after requests it. Usually spirit guides are deceased relatives, but this is not always the case. It can be anyone who has a vested interest in your well-being and happiness. You are not limited to one spirit guide. Their main concern is your spiritual growth. Consequently, your guides are prepared to help you discover your past lives, and will even guide you through the entire process if you wish.

It may feel as if you have just one spirit guide, but in practice, you have a number of guides looking after you. Whichever guide is appropriate to your current need will be available to help you at any given time.

Under normal circumstances you are not likely to see or hear your guide by using your eyes and ears. Guides communicate telepathically and it takes time and practice to become open to the messages they send. Often their messages will seem just like thoughts until you pause and think about them afterward. Because this is difficult for most people, various devices such as the Ouija board and automatic writing have been developed to make it easier to communicate with your guides.

Automatic Writing

Automatic writing became popular in the nineteenth century when spiritualists used it to communicate with the other side. However, it can be used for many purposes. A number of books have been written using automatic writing, for instance. One of the best examples of this is *Private Dowding* by W. T. Poole which became a bestseller in 1918. This book told of the experiences of Thomas Dowding, a young English schoolteacher who was killed by shrapnel in France. It provided comfort to many people who had lost their sons during the war.

Interestingly, Harriett Beecher Stowe, the celebrated author of *Uncle Tom's Cabin*, said, "She did not write it: it was given to her; it passed before her."[1] And in the preface to his famous poem "Jerusalem," William Blake wrote that the poem was dictated to him. T. P. James used automatic writing to complete *The Mystery of Edwin Drood*, which was unfinished when Charles Dickens died. And all of the works of Patience Worth were communicated by the Ouija board or automatic writing.[2]

Automatic writing is a natural phenomenon that anyone can do. However, it does take practice. Most people produce indecipherable shapes and letters when they start experimenting with automatic writing. However, with practice the writing becomes more and more legible.

All you need to do is sit down comfortably with a pad of paper and a pen or pencil. Your elbow should create an angle of ninety degrees. Hold the writing implement loosely in your hand, with the tip resting on the paper, and wait for it to move. Sit quietly and see what happens. The best results occur if you think about something else entirely and let the pen do whatever it wishes.

After a while the hand holding the pen will start to move. Pay no attention to this. Automatic writing is unconscious writing and this vital unconscious element is lost if you pay attention to what is being written.

If you are fortunate, you will start writing words and phrases immediately. Most people begin by drawing shapes such as circles and ellipses. You might write a few words in mirror writing. It does not matter what you produce to begin with. Practice regularly and your skill will develop. You will be amazed at what you produce. You will also discover that you can write for hours in this way without tiring. It is truly automatic writing.

You may find that you get better results by holding the pen in the hand that you do not usually write with.

This does not work for me, but I know several people who do all their automatic writing in this manner.

Once you have become familiar with the process, you can use automatic writing to explore your past lives. While you are sitting down waiting for the writing to begin, think about your desire to return to one of your past lives. You can think of a particular past life if you wish, or leave it to chance.

I prefer to use automatic writing to return to specific lifetimes that are connected with problems or difficulties in my present life. To do this, again while waiting for the pen to move, think about anything that is holding you back or blocking your progress in this lifetime.

Some years ago, one of my students stayed behind after the lesson to tell me that she had developed a phobia about going to church. Monica was a shy, retiring person who constantly fiddled with her handbag as she told me about her problem. Each time she went to church Monica found herself becoming more and more anxious. She thought she had found a solution by sitting at the back of the church near the door. Sitting here eased the tension, but did not eliminate it. Monica was a religious lady who enjoyed attending services, and was frustrated about no longer being able to attend church. I discovered that she had also stopped going to movies, or anywhere else where groups of people congregated. It seemed strange that she was able to come to my classes, but would not attend a movie. Monica explained that she had come to my classes only because her next-door neighbor wanted to come and assured her that I might be able to help her resolve this problem.

My first thought was to do a hypnotic regression, but I remembered how talented she was at automatic writing. I suggested that she use this method to return to whatever it was in the past that had caused this problem. The following week Monica returned with the answer.

The first time she tried to use automatic writing to find out the cause of the problem she became so tense that it did not work. Consequently, the following evening she had a couple of gin and tonics before commencing. It is not a practice I would have recommended, but it enabled Monica to relax enough to ensure that the procedure worked. She produced nonsense for the first few days, but persevered. Eventually she produced a strong message.

The pen wrote: "Very tired. No solution to problem. Marcus continues to abuse me night and day. No physical violence, but close. Constant mental abuse. Going to evening at Ranold's. Marcus forbids it, but going anyway. Twenty people there in small sitting room.

Ranold says prayers, then we sing John Wesley. Smoke. Smoke and fumes. House on fire and we rush for door, but it won't open. Blocked on outside. Run through house. Fall over. Can't breathe. Someone's pulling me. Too late. I'm at peace." (This was written as one long, continuous sentence. I have punctuated it, but have not altered the words.)

Monica had attended a church service a few days after receiving this message. She felt slightly nervous when she walked in, but was able to sit in the middle of the church and pay attention to the service. She left feeling better than she'd been for years.

Monica had no desire to explore that particular lifetime in more depth.

"I don't know who Marcus was, and I don't care," she told me. "I'm better off not knowing who he was."

Spirit Guide Regression

This is a progressive relaxation technique that allows your spirit guide to take you on an accompanied examination of your past lives. It was the favorite method of many of my students as it allowed them to see, and get to know, one of their spirit guides in the course of the regression.

As usual, make yourself comfortable in a reasonably warm room, and make sure that you will not be disturbed.

Step One—Relaxation

Take several deep breaths and exhale slowly. Allow all of your muscles to relax, starting with your toes and gradually working your way right up to the top of your head. When you feel that you are totally relaxed, mentally scan your body for any areas of tension. Relax them, and then scan again. When you feel completely relaxed, move on to step two.

Step Two—Meet Your Guide

Visualize yourself at the top of a beautiful staircase. I picture a magnificent marble staircase that I walked down many years ago in a chateau in France. Your staircase may be a real one or an imaginary one. It makes no difference, just as long as it is beautiful and has ten steps. You feel excited as you know that your spirit guide will be at the bottom of the staircase waiting to escort you back to a past life.

Place your hand on the handrail and slowly walk down the staircase, saying to yourself, "Ten, relax. . . . Nine, relax. . . . Eight, relax. . . ." and so on until you reach the bottom.

You realize that you have not yet met your spirit guide, but as you move out onto the floor of the most magnificent room you have ever seen, you see him or her walking toward you wearing a friendly smile (hereafter referred to as a male for simplicity). You feel that you have known your spirit guide for all of your life and you walk happily into his embrace. He then leads you to a comfortable sofa and the two of you sit down and discuss your desire to return to one of your past lives.

Step Three—Back Through Time

Your spirit guide listens to you with a gentle smile on his face. Every now and again he nods his head in agreement. When you have finished telling him which particular lifetime you want to return to, he indicates the doors leading off the room. Every one of these, he tells you, will lead you to one of your past lives. However, only one will lead you to the particular incarnation that you are wanting to explore.

Your spirit guide stands up and leads the way to a door on the far wall. He asks you if you are ready to proceed. He smiles at your positive answer, and opens the door.

It is impossible to see what is beyond the door as everything is blocked out by a dense mist. Your guide takes you by the hand and walks confidently inside. You hear the door close behind you.

You follow your guide deeper into the mist. He stops and asks you to listen. You hear faint sounds that you are unable to identify at first. But while you are still trying to identify them, the mist gradually fades away and you can look around.

Step Four—Explore Your Past Life

Once you become familiar with the scene, you can explore this past life in as much depth as you want. All you need to do is ask your spirit guide for whatever you want to see and it will instantly occur. For instance, if you want to see your partner in that past life, ask your spirit guide to take you to a scene involving him or her and it will immediately happen.

Likewise, when you are ready to return to the present, tell your spirit guide that you have had enough and instantly you will find yourself in the beautiful room where you first met him.

Step Five—Return to Full Conscious Awareness

Gradually become aware of the room and the realization that you are back in the present. Thank your spirit guide for the help and support, and climb slowly back up the stairs, counting from one to ten as you do so. When you feel ready, open your eyes, stretch, and get up.

Hillary's Experience

"I always felt a bit nervous about exploring my past lives," Hillary told me. She is a vivacious lady in her mid-thirties. As she seems extremely confident, I was surprised to hear her express her nervousness. "That's why I was excited to learn how to do it with my spirit guide. I had already made contact with him, so it made perfect sense to travel back in time with him."

Hillary went back to a past life in medieval times. "It must have been a nunnery," she said. "It was large—huge, actually—and we nuns led busy lives, praying, studying, and working. It was a satisfying life. The hard part was getting up in the middle of the night for matins and lauds. We got about eight hours sleep a night, that is if we went straight to bed at eight, but it was broken by the two o'clock service."

"Do any incidents in this life stand out?" I asked.

Hillary nodded. "Yes, a few actually. One was really surprising. About once a year the bishop would come to see how we were getting on. That was understandable, but what I didn't like was the way in which he got all the nuns to tattle on each other. We all saw him one at a time. He asked us questions while his clerk wrote everything down. The clerk had a permanent expression of shock on his face." Hillary closed her eyes to see the scene more vividly. "I didn't like it, so I never passed on any information. There were things I could've, and maybe should've, but it seemed wrong to tell tales about the people I spent every minute of my life with."

"Did the others tell tales?"

Hillary laughed. "Did they tell tales! They even made up stories about people they didn't like. Some made complaints about everyone."

"Not what you'd expect from a group of nuns."

Hillary shook her head. "We were just people. Some had a vocation, others didn't." Hillary sighed deeply. "There must have been a lot of karma gathered there! Anyway, I think saying nothing helped me in the end, because I became the prioress."

"Did you enjoy that?"

Hillary pondered the question. "Yes and no. I had my own rooms and a nun to help me. It was strange having a bit of privacy. Also, I went out a lot. I was suddenly running a business. I had to supervise the estates and check that no one was robbing us. It was hard work, especially when it was time to sell the wool, but some of the nuns resented me going out all the time. You can bet they told the bishop all about it on his visits!"

"Do you think so?"

Hillary snorted. "I know so. I was questioned each year by the bishop, the same as everyone else. I knew what was going on, and who liked me and who didn't. Some people resented the fact that I was prioress and spent all their time trying to undermine me and my authority. I was never able to relax completely. Still can't, actually."

"Is that a hangover from this past life?"

"Maybe. I'm not sure. What I do know is that I've never felt able to trust people. No matter what people say or do, I always wonder if they have another motive behind it. That definitely came from my life in the nunnery."

"Were you old when you died?"

Hillary nodded. "Very old, I think. I was still prioress. In fact, I outlived everyone who spoke against me. I think at the end I was respected. Maybe I was liked a bit too. I'm sure I wasn't loved."

"Why is that?"

"Because that whole life felt as if something important was missing. I had three sisters and I'd visit them and experience family life for a few days. I envied them their homes and husbands and families. I was the youngest in the family. That's why I became a nun. My sisters would come and stay with me at the nunnery too. That was the best time. I enjoyed that. I was happy then. The rest of the time I felt isolated, alone. Without love."

Hillary turned away and wiped her eyes. "Just like this lifetime."

I waited until she had regained her composure. "Will you change anything in your life as a result of this regression?"

Hillary squared her shoulders and looked directly at me. "I'm going to change everything!"

Spirit Guides Participating in the Regression

In my book *Spirit Guides and Angel Guardians,* I told the story of a client of mine who had a weight problem. During a hypnotherapy session she spontaneously regressed to a past life and met her spirit guide. She had been a man in that incarnation and his wife in that past life was her spirit guide in this lifetime.[3] Many people have experienced similar occurences.

As spirit guides are frequently deceased relatives, it is not surprising that they appear in so many people's past lives. Everyone I know who has experienced this has taken the presence of their spirit guide for granted. They found it a highly positive experience to be able to see their spirit guides in this way. This is usually the first time that these people have seen their spirit guides, and they find the experience comforting and helpful. In fact, the appearance and recognition of a spirit guide is usually the most important aspect of the regression, no matter how exciting the rest of the memories are.

Unfortunately, you cannot guarantee that you will regress back to a previous life and make contact with your spirit guide. Some people have experimented by suggesting before the regression that they will return to a lifetime that includes their spirit guide. Unfortunately, the results have been inconclusive. All you can do is remain alert to the possibility. You will have no problems in recognizing your spirit guide. Everyone who has experienced this told me that recognition was instant, and often overpowering.

Although you may not meet your spirit guide in the course of a normal regression, you can always ask your spirit guide to accompany you whenever you wish.

Afterword

I shall return to thee,
Earth, O dearest
Mother of mine!
I who have loved thee with joy everlasting,
Endless discovery, newness diurnal . . .
Now I depart . . .
I shall still blindly fumble and wait
'Till the true door opens, the true voice call again;
And back to the human high estate,
Back to the whole of the soul, resurgent,
O Earth! O dearest! I shall return,
I shall return to thee, Earth, my mother.

Margaret L. Woods (1856–1945)

When you accept the concept of reincarnation you have the opportunity to transform your life. Some people claim that if you accept reincarnation and karma, you need not make any effort and can just accept life as it is. Of course, the opposite is the case. You are much more likely to lead a good, productive life when you accept reincarnation, as you will be aware that all karma, good or bad, will be paid back eventually. This means that you will take full responsibility for your actions and the way in which you live your life. Your relationships with others will improve because you will be more caring, sympathetic, and understanding of others. By becoming aware of your own actions you are much less likely to be malicious, dishonest, or spiteful. Shaw Desmond explained this succinctly when he wrote, "The knowledge that if one wrongs a woman in this life he will assuredly have to reckon with her in a future life makes one think!"[1]

Once you have unlocked the memory banks of your previous incarnations, you will also be kinder to yourself. You will understand that you are the way you are because of everything you have done in the past. In other words, you have earned your present position in life. And the kind of future you want for yourself depends on your thoughts and actions in this lifetime.

You will learn that every moment of life is valuable. Nothing is wasted. Your times of sadness are just as important in the scheme of things as your moments of supreme happiness and fulfillment. Everything plays a part in your progress and development.

Learning about your past lives shows you what lessons need to be focused on in this incarnation. They also reveal your strengths. Most people tend to underrate themselves. Discovering how they handled difficult situations in previous lifetimes frequently raises people's self-esteem, and makes them realize that they are much better people than they thought they were.

Remember to enjoy yourself while investigating your many past lives. Relax and have fun. You are not likely to achieve good results if you are worried, overly stressed, skeptical, depressed, or overtired. You will be most successful when you feel positive, expectant, and open-minded.

Be patient. I know you will be successful in time. However, everyone is different. Some people return to their past lives immediately, while other people need to practice for a long time. It is natural to become disheartened and disappointed when it takes longer than expected to achieve success. In the fast-moving world of today, we all want instant results. Unfortunately, this seldom occurs when investigating past lives. If you are having difficulty, take time out for some fun activities and return to your past lives when you are feeling relaxed and happy.

I know you will learn a great deal about yourself by examining your past lives. I hope the information in this book will help you discover lessons that need to be learned, and will enable you to enjoy a happy, fulfilled, and successful future.

Notes

Chapter 1

1. Story, *The Case for Rebirth*, 1.
2. Iamblichus, *Life of Pythagoras*, 4.17.
3. Walker, *Masks of the Soul*, 32–33.
4. Plato, *Laws*, 155.
5. References to reincarnation in the Bible include Job 4:8, Prov. 8:22–31, Eccles. 1:9–11, Mal. 4:5, Matt. 16:13–14, Matt. 17:9–13, Matt. 11:11–15, Mark 9:13, Rom. 9:10–13, and Rev. 3:12. Also, the Apocrypha is found in Roman Catholic editions of the Bible. In the Apocrypha, The Wisdom of Solomon 8:19–20, we read, "Now I was a child

good by nature, and a good soul fell to my lot. Nay, rather, being good, I came into a body undefiled."

6. Head and Cranston, *Reincarnation,* 99.
7. *Yalkut Re'uveni* (trans. Fitzgerald), nos. 1, 8, 61, 63.
8. *Zohar* (trans. Sperling and Simon), 2:99.
9. *The Koran* (trans. Rodwell), 2:28, 5:60, 71:17–18.
10. Langley, *Edgar Cayce on Reincarnation,* 10.
11. Wambach, *Reliving Past Lives,* 125.
12. Currie, *You Cannot Die,* 292.
13. Stevenson, *Where Reincarnation and Biology Intersect,* 1.
14. My account of Parmod's life is taken from a number of published sources: Atreya, *Introduction to Parapsychology,* 116–21; Story, *The Case for Rebirth,* 25–31; Stevenson, *Twenty Cases Suggestive of Reincarnation,* 109–27; Stemman, *Reincarnation,* 82–83.
15. Gerard, *DNA Healing Techniques,* 17.
16. Steiger, *You Will Live Again,* 33–48.

Chapter 3

1. Humphreys, *Karma and Rebirth,* 38.
2. Cited quotations come from the King James Version. Other references to karma in the Bible include Gen. 9:6; Deut. 24:12; Hos. 8:7; Hos. 10:13; Ps. 9:16; Ps. 62:12; Prov. 24:12; Jer. 17:10; Jer. 32:19; Ezek. 18:20; Ezek. 18:30; Matt. 5:18; Matt. 7:1–2; Matt. 7:12; Matt. 7:17; Matt. 16:27; Luke 16:17; Rom. 2:6; Rom. 2:9–13; Rom. 14:12; 2 Cor. 5:10; 1 Pet. 1:17; Rev. 20:12; Rev. 22:12.
3. Fisher, *The Case for Reincarnation,* 128–33. See also Whitton and Fisher, *Life Between Life.*
4. Emerson, *Lectures and Biographical Sketches,* 121.
5. Jung, *Memories, Dreams, Reflections,* 294.

Chapter 4

1. Tart, foreword to *Control Your Dreams*, vii.
2. Armitage, Rochlen, and Finch, "Dream Recall and Major Depression," 8–14. Quoted in Moss, *Conscious Dreaming*, 35.
3. *The New Encyclopaedia Britannica: Macropaedia, Knowledge in Depth*, 15th ed., s. v. "Dreams."
4. Information about R.E.M. sleep comes from *Many Lifetimes* by Grant and Kelsey.
5. Langley, *Edgar Cayce on Reincarnation*, 75.
6. There are many books available on dream yoga. Two of the best are *Tibetan Yoga and Secret Doctrines* by W. Y. Evans-Wentz and *Dream Yoga and the Practice of Natural Light* by Namkai Norbu.

Chapter 9

1. Henry Ford, interview.
2. Weatherhead, *Life Begins at Death*, 72.
3. Viviane's experiences have been written up in many places. The most readable source is *The Unknown Power* by Guy Lyon Playfair.
4. Stemman, *Reincarnation*, 179.

Chapter 10

1. Webster, *Dowsing for Beginners*, 11.
2. Ibid., xiii.
3. Mermet, *Principles and Practice of Radiesthesia*, 207–8.

Chapter 12

1. Desmond, *Reincarnation for Everyman*, 98–109.

Chapter 13

1. Moss and Keeton, *Encounters with the Past,* 16.
2. Averroes, *On the Soul,* 121.
3. Langley, *Edgar Cayce on Reincarnation,* 47.

Chapter 15

1. Fodor, *Encyclopaedia of Psychic Science,* 22.
2. Webster, *Spirit Guides and Angel Guardians,* 172–75.
3. Ibid., 273–77.

Afterword

1. Desmond, *Reincarnation for Everyman,* 39.

Bibliography and Suggested Reading

Algeo, John. *Reincarnation Explored*. Wheaton, Ill.: The Theosophical Publishing House, 1987.

Andrews, Ted. *How to Uncover Your Past Lives*. St. Paul, Minn.: Llewellyn Publications, 1992.

Armitage, Roseanne, Aaron Rochlen, and Thomas Finch. "Dream Recall and Major Depression," 8–14. Paper presented at the eleventh conference of the Association for the Study of Dreams, Leiden, the Netherlands, 1994. Quoted in Robert Moss, *Conscious Dreaming* (New York: Crown Trade Paperbacks, 1996), 35.

Atreya, B. L. *Introduction to Parapsychology*. Benares, India: The International Standard Publications, 1957.

Auerbach, Loyd. *Psychic Dreaming*. New York: Warner Books, Inc., 1991.

———. *Reincarnation, Channeling and Possession*. New York: Warner Books, Inc., 1993.

Averroes (Ibn Rushd). *On the Soul*. Trans. W. Emmanuel. N.p.: 1822.

Bernstein, Morey. *The Search for Bridey Murphy*. New York: Doubleday and Company, 1956.

Billing, Philip B. *My First Incarnation with the Maori People*. Te Kawhata, New Zealand: Mitaki Ra Publications, 1997.

Blythe, Henry. *The Three Lives of Naomi Henry*. London: Frederick Muller Limited, 1956.

Brennan, J. H. *Reincarnation: Five Keys to Past Lives*. Rev. ed. Wellingborough, England: The Aquarian Press, 1981.

Castaneda, Carlos. *Journey to Ixtlan: The Lessons of Don Juan*. New York: Simon & Schuster, Inc., 1972.

Cerminara, Gina. *Many Lives, Many Loves*. Marina del Rey, Calif.: DeVorss and Company, 1963.

Cockell, Jenny. *Yesterday's Children*. London: Judy Piatkus Publishers Limited, 1993.

Cooper, Irving S. *Reincarnation: The Hope of the World*. London: The Theosophical Publishing House, 1918.

Cott, Jonathan. *The Search for Omm Sety*. New York: Doubleday and Company, 1987.

Cranston, Sylvia, and Carey Williams. *Reincarnation: A New Horizon in Science, Religion and Society*. New York: Julian Press, 1984.

Currie, Ian. *You Cannot Die.* Rockport, Mass.: Element Books, 1995.

Desmond, Shaw. *Reincarnation for Everyman.* London: Rider and Company, 1950.

Dowding, Lord Hugh. *Lychgate: The Entrance to the Path.* London: Rider and Company Limited, 1945.

Edwards, Paul. *Reincarnation: A Critical Examination.* Amherst, N.Y.: Prometheus Books, 1996.

Emerson, Ralph Waldo. *Lectures and Biographical Sketches.* 1868. Reprint, London: The Philosophical Learning Foundation, 1923.

Evans-Wentz, W. Y. *Tibetan Yoga and Secret Doctrines.* New York: Oxford University Press, 1958.

Fisher, Joe. *The Case for Reincarnation.* Toronto: Somerville House Publishing, 1984.

Fodor, Nandor. *Encyclopaedia of Psychic Science.* New York: University Books, Inc., 1974.

Ford, Henry. Interview by George Sylvester Viereck. *San Francisco Examiner,* 26 August 1928.

Gallup, George, with William Proctor. *Adventures in Immortality.* New York: McGraw-Hill Book Company, 1982.

Gater, Dilys. *Past Lives: Case Histories of Previous Existence.* London: Robert Hale Limited, 1997.

Gerard, Robert V., Ph.D. *DNA Healing Techniques.* 3d ed. Coarsegold, Calif.: Oughten House Foundation, Inc., 1999.

Goldberg, Bruce, Dr. *Past Lives, Future Lives.* North Hollywood, Calif.: Newcastle Publishing Company, Inc., 1982.

Gordon, Henry. *Channeling into the New Age: The Teachings of Shirley MacLaine and Other Such Gurus.* Buffalo, N.Y.: Prometheus Books, 1988.

Grant, Joan. *Winged Pharaoh*. London: Arthur Baker Limited, 1937.

Grant, Joan, and Denys Kelsey. *Many Lifetimes*. New York: Doubleday and Company, 1967.

Green, Celia. *Lucid Dreams*. London: Hamish Hamilton Limited, 1968.

Guirdham, Arthur. *The Cathars and Reincarnation*. London: Turnstone Press, 1970.

Hartley, Christine. *The Case for Reincarnation*. London: Robert Hale Limited, 1986.

Head, Joseph, and S. L. Cranston, eds. *Reincarnation: An East-West Anthology*. Wheaton, Ill.: The Theosophical Publishing House, 1968.

Hughes, Thea Stanley. *Twentieth Century Question: Reincarnation*. Somerton, England: Movement Publications, 1979.

Hanson, V., R. Stewart, and S. Nicholson. *Karma: Rhythmic Return to Harmony*. Wheaton, Ill.: The Theosophical Publishing House, 1990.

Humphreys, Christmas. *Karma and Rebirth*. London: John Murray Limited, 1943.

Iamblichus. *Life of Pythagoras, or Pythagoric Life*. N.p.: A. J. Valpy, 1818.

Iverson, Jeffrey. *More Lives Than One*. London: Souvenir Press, 1976.

Jung, Carl. *Memories, Dreams, Reflections*. London: Collins and Routledge and Kegan Paul, 1963.

Kason, Yvonne, and Teri Degler. *A Farther Shore*. Toronto: HarperCollins Publishers Ltd., 1994.

Langley, Noel. *Edgar Cayce on Reincarnation*. New York: Castle Books, 1967.

Lenz, Frederick, Dr. *Lifetimes*. New York: Bobbs-Merrill Company, 1979.

Linn, Denise. *Past Lives, Present Dreams*. London: Judy Piatkus Publishers Limited, 1994.

Luntz, Charles E. *The Challenge of Reincarnation*. St. Louis, Mo.: Charles E. Luntz Publications, 1957.

MacLaine, Shirley. *Out on a Limb*. London: Elm Tree Books, 1983.

McClain, Florence Wagner. *A Practical Guide to Past Life Regression*. St. Paul, Minn.: Llewellyn Publications, 1985.

Mermet, Abbé. *Principles and Practice of Radiesthesia*. Trans. Mark Clement. 1959. Reprint, Longmead, Dorset, England: Element Books, 1987.

Moore, Marcia. *Hypersentience*. New York: Crown Publishers, Inc., 1976.

Moss, Peter, and Joe Keeton. *Encounters with the Past*. London: Sidgwick and Jackson Limited, 1979.

Mumford, Jonn, Dr. *Karma Manual*. St. Paul, Minn.: Llewellyn Publications, 1999.

Newton, Michael. *Journey of Souls*. St. Paul, Minn.: Llewellyn Publications, 1994.

Norbu, Namkai. *Dream Yoga and the Practice of Natural Light*. Ithaca, N.Y.: Snow Lion, Inc., 1992.

Perkins, James S. *Experiencing Reincarnation*. Wheaton, Ill.: The Theosophical Publishing House, 1977.

Plato. *The Laws*. Trans. A. D. Lindsay. London: J. M. Dent and Sons Limited, 1912.

Playfair, Guy Lyon. *The Unknown Power*. New York: Pocket Books, 1975.

Poole, W. T. *Private Dowding*. London: Rider and Company, 1918.

Rogo, D. Scott. *Life After Death: The Case for Survival of Bodily Death*. Wellingborough, England: The Aquarian Press, 1986.

————. *The Search for Yesterday: A Critical Examination of the Evidence for Reincarnation*. Englewood Cliffs, N.J.: Prentice Hall and Company, 1985.

Rolfe, Mona. *The Spiral of Life: Cycles of Reincarnation*. 1975. Reprint, Saffron Walden, England: The C. W. Daniel Company Limited, 1992.

Rosen, Steven. *The Reincarnation Controversy*. Badger, Calif.: Torchlight Publishing, Inc., 1997.

de Saint-Denys, Marquis d'Hervey. *Les Reves et les Moyens de les diriger*. Paris: Amyot, 1867.

Sarris, Arian. *Healing the Past*. St. Paul, Minn.: Llewellyn Publications, 1997.

Scholem, Gershom, ed. *Zohar, The Book of Splendor: Basic Readings from the Kabbalah*. New York: Schoken Books, 1974.

Sharma, I. C. *Cayce, Karma and Reincarnation*. Wheaton, Ill.: The Theosophical Publishing House, 1982.

Stearn, Jess. *The Search for the Girl with the Blue Eyes*. Garden City, N.Y.: Doubleday and Company, 1968.

Steiger, Brad. *You Will Live Again*. Nevada City, Calif.: Blue Dolphin Publishing, Inc., 1996.

Steiner, Rudolf. *Reincarnation and Immortality*. Blauvelt, N.Y.: Multimedia Publishing Corporation, 1970.

Stemman, Roy. *Reincarnation: Amazing True Cases from Around the World*. London: Judy Piatkus Publishers Limited, 1997.

Stevenson, Ian, Dr. *Children Who Remember Previous Lives.* Charlottesville, Va.: The University Press of Virginia, 1987.

———. *Twenty Cases Suggestive of Reincarnation.* 2d ed. Charlottesville, Va.: The University Press of Virginia, 1974.

———. *Where Reincarnation and Biology Intersect.* Westport, Conn.: Praeger Publishers, 1997.

Story, Francis. *The Case for Rebirth.* Kandy, Sri Lanka: Buddhist Publication Society, 1959.

Street, Noel. *The Man Who Can Look Backward.* New York: Samuel Weiser, Inc., 1969.

Tart, Charles T., Dr. Foreword to *Control Your Dreams,* by Jayne Gackenbach and Jane Bosveld. New York: Harper and Row Publishers, Inc., 1989.

Vallieres, Ingrid. *Reincarnation Therapy.* Trans. Pat Campbell. Bath, England: Ashgrove Press, 1991.

Van Auken, John. *Born Again and Again: How Reincarnation Occurs and What It Means to You.* Virginia Beach, Va.: Inner Vision Publishing Company, 1984.

Walker, Benjamin. *Masks of the Soul: The Facts Behind Reincarnation.* Wellingborough, England: The Aquarian Press, 1981.

Walker, E. D. *Reincarnation: A Study of Forgotten Truth.* 1888. Reprint, New Hyde Park, N.Y.: University Books, Inc., 1965.

Wambach, Helen. *Reliving Past Lives: The Evidence Under Hypnosis.* New York: Harper and Row Publishers, Inc., 1978.

Watson, Lyall. *The Romeo Error.* Garden City, N.Y.: Anchor Press/Doubleday, 1975.

Weatherhead, Leslie D. *Life Begins at Death.* Nashville, Tenn.: Abingdon Press, 1969.

Webster, Richard. *Dowsing for Beginners.* St. Paul, Minn.: Llewellyn Publications, 1996.

———. *Numerology Magic.* St. Paul, Minn.: Llewellyn Publications, 1995.

———. *Spirit Guides and Angel Guardians.* St. Paul, Minn.: Llewellyn Publications, 1998.

Weiss, Brian L. *Many Lives, Many Masters.* New York: Simon and Schuster Inc., 1989.

———. *Only Love Is Real.* New York: Warner Books, Inc., 1996.

Whitton, Joel L., and Joe Fisher. *Life Between Life: A Scientific Exploration into the Void Separating One Incarnation from the Next.* New York: Doubleday and Company, 1986.

Williams, Loring G. "Reincarnation of a Civil War Victim." *Fate* 19 (December 1966): 44–58.

Winkler, E. Arthur, Dr. *Reincarnation and the Interim Between Lives.* Cottonwood, Ariz.: Esoteric Publications, 1976.

Yalkut Re'uveni. Trans. W. Fitzgerald. London: G. Wilberforce, 1837.

Zohar: The Book of Splendor. Trans. Harry Sperling and Maurice Simon. London: N.p., 1931–34.

Index

REACH FOR THE MOON

Llewellyn publishes hundreds of books on your favorite subjects! To get these exciting books, including the ones on the following pages, check your local bookstore or order them directly from Llewellyn.

Order by Phone
- Call toll-free within the U.S. and Canada, 1-800-THE MOON
- In Minnesota, call (651) 291-1970
- We accept VISA, MasterCard, and American Express

Order by Mail
- Send the full price of your order (MN residents add 7% sales tax) in U.S. funds, plus postage & handling to:

  Llewellyn Worldwide
  P.O. Box 64383, Dept. 0-7387-0077-0
  St. Paul, MN 55164–0383, U.S.A.

Postage & Handling
- **Standard** (U.S., Mexico, & Canada)

If your order is:

$20.00 or under, add $5.00

$20.01–$100.00, add $6.00

Over $100, shipping is free

(Continental U.S. orders ship UPS. AK, HI, PR, & P.O. Boxes ship USPS 1st class. Mex. & Can. ship PMB.)

- **Second Day Air** (Continental U.S. only): $10.00 for one book + $1.00 per each additional book
- **Express** (AK, HI, & PR only) [Not available for P.O. Box delivery. For street address delivery only.]: $15.00 for one book + $1.00 per each additional book
- **International Surface Mail:** Add $1.00 per item
- **International Airmail:** Books—Add the retail price of each item; Non-book items—Add $5.00 per item

Please allow 4–6 weeks for delivery on all orders.
Postage and handling rates subject to change.

Discounts
We offer a 20% discount to group leaders or agents. You must order a minimum of 5 copies of the same book to get our special quantity price.

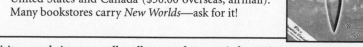

FREE CATALOG
Get a free copy of our color catalog, *New Worlds of Mind and Spirit*. Subscribe for just $10.00 in the United States and Canada ($30.00 overseas, airmail). Many bookstores carry *New Worlds*—ask for it!

Visit our website at www.llewellyn.com for more information.

Astral Travel for Beginners

Transcend Time and Space with Out-of-Body Experiences

RICHARD WEBSTER

Astral projection, or out-of-body travel, is a completely natural experience. You have already astral traveled thousands of times in your sleep, you just don't remember it when you wake up. Now, you can learn how to leave your body at will, be fully conscious of the experience, and remember it when you return.

The exercises in this book are carefully graded to take you step-by-step through an actual out-of-body experience. Once you have accomplished this, it becomes easier and easier to leave your body. That's why the emphasis in this book is on your first astral travel.

The ability to astral travel can change your life. You will have the freedom to go anywhere and do anything. You can explore new worlds, go back and forth through time, make new friends, and even find a lover on the astral planes. Most importantly, you will find that you no longer fear death as you discover that you are indeed a spiritual being independent of your physical body.

1-56718-796-X
256 pp., 5³⁄₁₆ x 8   **$9.95**

To order, call 1-800-THE MOON
Prices subject to change without notice